Practice Tests for IGCSE English as a Second Language

Reading and Writing
Book 1

Previously published by Georgian Press

Marian Barry,
Barbara Campbell,
Sue Daish

CAMBRIDGE
UNIVERSITY PRESS

University Printing House, Cambridge CB2 8BS, United Kingdom

Cambridge University Press is part of the University of Cambridge.

It furthers the University's mission by disseminating knowledge in the pursuit of education, learning and research at the highest international levels of excellence.

www.cambridge.org
Information on this title: www.cambridge.org/9780521140591 (without key)
www.cambridge.org/9780521140614 (with key)

© Marian Barry, Barbara Campbell and Sue Daish 2006

First published by Georgian Press (Jersey) Limited 2006
Second edition 2007
Reprinted and published by Cambridge University Press 2010
7th printing 2014

A catalogue record for this publication is available from the British Library

ISBN 978-0-521-14059-1 Paperback without key
ISBN 978-0-521-14061-4 Paperback without key

® IGCSE is the registered trademark of Cambridge International Examinations

Produced by AMR Design Ltd (www.amrdesign.com)

Cover image © Pic and Mix Images/Alamy

ACKNOWLEDGEMENTS

The authors and publishers acknowledge the following sources of copyright material and are grateful for the permissions granted. While every effort has been made, it has not always been possible to identify the sources of all the material used, or to trace all copyright holders. If any omissions are brought to our notice we will be happy to include the appropriate acknowledgement on reprinting.

The Daily Telegraph for 'The tough grass that sweetens our lives' by Sanjida O'Connell (page 22), © Telegraph Group London 2004.

Nicola Day for 'Time to get drinking!' (page 56).

The Deep for their publicity material (page 20).

Dinosaur Farm for their publicity material (page 66).

Euro Space Center for their publicity material (page 34).

The Independent for 'Scruffy, seedy and sorely needed: why decline of India's vultures has become a threat to public health' by Michael McCarthy, 4.2.03, (page 72) and 'English to be spoken by half the world's population within 10 years' by James Burleigh, 9.12.04, (page 68), © The Independent.

The Lady magazine for 'The invisible scent' by Arline Usden (page 58).

Victoria McKee for 'Colour therapy' (page 74).

New Scientist for 'Born to trade' by Kate Douglas (page 42).

Saga magazine for 'The gentlest giant' by Nigel Blundell (page 52).

The Sunday Express for 'Why dolphins seem intent on proving that they are man's best friend' by Stuart Winter (page 26), © Express Newspapers 2004.

Waitrose Food Illustrated for 'Hive Aid' by Ben de Pear (page 36) and 'Watercress' by Liz Franklin (page 40).

Illustrations by David Woodroffe (pages 20, 36, 52, 60) and AMR Design (pages 22, 68)

Photographs by permission of Corbis (pages 22, 26, 40, 56, 58) and Robert Harvey (pages 42, 52, 72)

CONTENTS

PAPER 1   Reading and Writing

(Core curriculum) $1\frac{1}{2}$ hours

PAPER 2   Reading and Writing

(Extended curriculum)   2 hours

EXERCISE 1: READING

Candidates answer questions of factual detail about a text (an advertisement, brochure, leaflet, guide, instructions, etc). Skimming/scanning and gist reading skills are tested, and short answers using single words or phrases are required.

Total marks: Core 6, Extended 8

EXERCISE 2: READING

Candidates answer questions requiring a more detailed understanding of a text, such as a report or newspaper/magazine article with a graphical element (a map, chart, graph or diagram). One question may ask candidates to make a list of points based on the text.

Total marks: Core 10, Extended 14

EXERCISE 3: INFORMATION TRANSFER

Candidates complete a form or skeletal notes using information given in a scenario on the question paper.

Total marks: Core 10, Extended 8

EXERCISE 4: NOTE-MAKING

Candidates write brief notes from a written text, under a heading or headings provided.

Total marks: Core 6, Extended 8

EXERCISE 5: SUMMARY WRITING

Extended candidates write about 100 words on an aspect or aspects of a written text, such as a newspaper or magazine article.

Core candidates write a paragraph of no more than 70 words, using their notes from Exercise 4.

Total marks: Core 4, Extended 10

EXERCISE 6: WRITING

Extended candidates write about 150-200 words (Core candidates 100-150 words) of continuous prose. The purpose, format and audience are specified, e.g. an informal letter to a friend, or an article about a holiday for the school magazine. Candidates must use an appropriate style and register. A stimulus is provided, in the form of pictures or photos and/or short prompts.

Total marks: Core 10, Extended 18

EXERCISE 7: WRITING

Extended candidates write about 150-200 words (Core candidates 100-150 words) of continuous prose. The format, purpose and audience are specified, and will be different from Exercise 6, e.g. a formal letter to a newspaper about a local issue. Candidates must use an appropriate style and register. A stimulus is provided, in the form of pictures or photos and/or short prompts.

The prompts are a guide to help students focus their thoughts and are not meant to be prescriptive. Good candidates can use them selectively, and some may choose to write totally without reference to the prompts. This is perfectly acceptable, as long as they do not drift away from the point of the question.

Total marks: Core 10, Extended 18

TOTAL MARKS FOR PAPER 1: 56
Weighting: 70%   **Grades available:** C-G

TOTAL MARKS FOR PAPER 2: 84
Weighting: 70%   **Grades available:** A-E

PAPER 3   Listening

(Core curriculum)   30–40 minutes

PAPER 4   Listening

(Extended curriculum)   45 minutes

QUESTIONS 1–6

Candidates answer questions on six short spoken texts, such as informal conversations, travel announcements, answerphone messages. They are required to identify specific points of information. Each text is heard twice, and short answers (one word or phrase) are required.
Total marks: Core 7, Extended 8

QUESTIONS 7 AND 8

Candidates listen to two recordings of longer spoken texts, such as formal or informal conversations, interviews, monologues, formal talks. Each text is heard twice.

Candidates fill in skeletal notes or close gaps on forms or charts with single words or short phrases. They need to be able to select information from what may be incidental.
Total marks: Core 12, Extended 16

QUESTIONS 9 AND 10

Candidates listen to two recordings, which may be informal conversations or more formal talks, interviews, etc. Each text is heard twice.

Extended candidates answer about six questions on each recording, requiring short or sentence-length answers. Core candidates answer about 10 true-false or multiple-choice questions on each recording by ticking boxes. In both cases, candidates need to be able to understand more complex meanings, opinions and attitudes of the speakers. Extended candidates should also be able to infer meaning implicit in the text.
Total marks: Core 11, Extended 12

TOTAL MARKS FOR PAPER 3: 30
Weighting: 30%   **Grades available:** C–G

TOTAL MARKS FOR PAPER 4: 36
Weighting: 30%   **Grades available:** A–E

COMPONENT 5 Oral test

(Core and Extended curriculum) 10–12 mins

Candidates take part in a discussion with the teacher/examiner, and possibly another candidate, on a set topic. There are up to five topics, e.g. holidays, health and fitness, the rights and wrongs of zoos, winning the lottery. After a short warm-up, which is not assessed, candidates are allowed 2–3 minutes to read the Oral Assessment card which has been selected by the examiner. The cards include prompts to guide the discussion. Candidates are not allowed to make written notes.

The conversation itself should last 6-9 minutes.

Detailed guidance is provided by CIE on how to conduct the Oral tests, and advice should be sought regarding all aspects of the tests.
Grades available: 1 (high) to 5 (low)

COMPONENT 6 Oral coursework

(Core and Extended curriculum)

Instead of Component 5, centres may, with the permission of CIE, opt for Component 6. This is a coursework option in which oral work is set and assessed by the teacher, at any time in the year before the written exam. Each candidate is assessed on three oral tasks, e.g. role play situations, telephone conversations, interviews, paired or group discussions, brief talks followed by discussion, debates. Further guidance on suitable types of tasks is given in the Distance Training Pack, available from CIE.
Grades available: 1 (high) to 5 (low)

More detailed information about the IGCSE in E2L examination, including support available for teachers, can be obtained from University of Cambridge International Examinations, 1 Hills Road, Cambridge CB1 2EU, United Kingdom, and online at **www.cie.org.uk**

About the IGCSE in E2L

These Practice Tests are designed to give practice in the Reading and Writing papers of the revised (2006) Cambridge IGCSE examination in English as Second Language. The exam is set at two levels, known as Core and Extended. The Core papers are aimed at lower-intermediate to intermediate students, hoping to achieve a grade C–G, while the Extended level is for intermediate to upper-intermediate students hoping to achieve grades A*–E. *(See IGCSE in E2L at a Glance on pages 6/7 for a detailed overview.)*

The exam is usually taken as part of the IGCSE curriculum, which offers a wide range of subjects. It can be taken at any age, although most students are about 16 years old. Students generally study for the exam over a period of two years, which allows them to develop both intellectually and emotionally.

The IGCSE in E2L qualification is widely recognised by universities where evidence of attainment in English is a requirement of entry.

About the Practice Tests

Like the exam, the material used in the Practice Tests aims to be international in perspective, culturally fair to students from all parts of the world, educational in impact and to reflect the needs and interests of teenagers. Exam tasks are realistic and similar to what students could be expected to meet at work, in training or in academic study.

The **Practice Tests** have the following benefits:

- They introduce students to the exam format.

- They allow students to experience a simulated exam under exam-type conditions.

- They help to build confidence and to develop exam techniques.

- Gaps in students' learning and skills can be uncovered and remedied.

- Students can acquire insight into what the examiners are looking for.

Common questions asked about the IGCSE in E2L

Why are there two choices of entry level?
The separate papers for Core and Extended levels are intended to encompass a wide ability range and to allow all students a chance of being awarded a qualification and a grade which reflects their level of ability in English.

This book contains three Extended-level Practice Tests (the most popular level) and one Core-level Test.

What are the differences between Papers 1 and 2? (i.e. Reading and Writing, Core, and Reading and Writing, Extended)
The exercises and tasks for the two levels are very similar. The differences are largely in the way the same exercises are adapted to be more challenging at Extended level and to stretch the candidates further. This is achieved mainly by asking additional questions on a reading text or by asking Extended candidates to write at greater length. However, there are a few specific differences. At Core level, note-taking and summary tasks are based on one text, whereas at Extended level, two different texts are used and the tasks are kept completely separate.

Some of the exam-type texts look very demanding. Is this a real problem?
Although some exam-type texts are demanding in terms of reading level, the tasks which students are asked to carry out in the exam are very straightforward. Exam practice will build the necessary confidence required to tackle difficult-looking texts with assurance.

I notice there is no Use of English paper in the exam. Why is this?
The aim of the exam is to enable students to make the language that they know work effectively in a practical context. The testing of language structures and vocabulary is integrated into the assessment of students' ability to carry out practical communication tasks. A few slight technical mistakes will not affect a student's grade as long as the overall impression is appropriate. This approach is fairer to students learning English in a second-language situation, where they may be 'picking up' English in a number of ways, not just learning it in their English classes.

How to use the Practice Tests

The Tests are designed to be used as flexibly as possible. They can be introduced at any time in the learning process when you feel students will benefit from being tested on exam-style exercises. Tests may be broken down into stand-alone exercises and integrated into coursework, perhaps as consolidation for work on a particular skill. Some exercises could be discussed in class before students start work on them; others could be treated as a check on skill level and students asked to complete them without help. The latter approach is also useful for diagnostic assessment at the start of the course. Alternatively, a whole test could be taken as a mock exam under exam conditions when you feel the students are ready. Obviously, you may have to extend normal lesson time to do this. Test results should help predict the kind of grade the students will get in the exam itself.

Timing

One of the benefits of Practice Tests is that students have the opportunity to practise timing themselves to see how they can build up speed for the actual exam. You can help them do this by gradually reducing the amount of time you allocate to particular exercises. This will encourage them to sustain concentration at a higher level for longer periods, to read and retain information more effectively, and to produce writing of a better and more consistent quality.

General advice on marking

When you decide on a mark, you need to take into account how well the student has completed the particular task. Students who fulfil a task very effectively should be given either full or very high marks. Students who do less well should naturally be awarded lower marks. However, the extent to which you apply this criterion will depend on the needs and capabilities of your own students. In order to motivate and encourage, you may want to be quite lenient in grading work at first, when the exercises are relatively unfamiliar, and become stricter as students progress in skills and experience.

Marking comprehension exercises

The right answer to a comprehension question is one in which the student has extracted the correct information from the text. An answer to a question may also be drawn from non-verbal information such as a chart or graph.

Sometimes there is more than one possible answer to a question. This is shown in the Key by the use of slash/slashes. Information which may be included in the answer but which is not necessary for achieving the mark is put into brackets. Answers requiring specific amounts, percentages, numbers, etc must be exact, not generalised. Sometimes an answer to a question has more than one element and both elements are required to obtain the mark. This is shown clearly both in the layout of the question and in the Key.

Marking information transfer (form-filling) exercises

Look out for the most common exam mistakes, which are:

- Filling in the form for themselves, not the person in the scenario.

- Mistakes in copying factual details (e.g. names, addresses, telephone numbers, dates), which need to be error-free to obtain the marks allocated.

- Not using block capital letters where required.

- Not following specific instructions such as *Circle*, *Delete*, *Tick*, etc.

Marking note-taking exercises

In the exam, the note-taking exercises take the form of headings followed by bullet points, against which students write their notes. Full sentences are not required and answers can be one word or a brief phrase. Students should take care with spelling, however, as they may inadvertently miss a mark if a misspelled word gives another meaning. The bullet points guide the student as to the number of points to find, and each point should be used only once.

Weak note-taking answers tend to extract irrelevant information from the text or put the right points under the wrong headings.

Marking summaries

Summary questions are selective which means that only some of the information in the text is relevant.

Core-level summaries are linked to the preceding note-taking task. Students are asked to re-present their notes in continuous prose. For example, in Exercise 4 the students may make notes for a wildlife club on a text about endangered species. Then, in Exercise 5, they have to summarise the notes into a connected paragraph for a school magazine feature. The summary exercise for Extended-level is completely separate from the preceding note-taking exercise.

When marking summaries look for the following:

- Inclusion of the appropriate content points.

- The ability to change some of the language of the text into own words without destroying the original meaning.

- Use of a clear and logical sequence.

- Good spelling, grammar and punctuation.

Good summaries should be completely understandable, even by someone who has not seen the original text. Weaker summaries, on the other hand, show less understanding of the task by failing to include all the relevant points. Weaker answers often include information which is not required by the question, chunks of text are copied, and there are errors in grammar and vocabulary which obscure the meaning.

Detailed guidelines for marking the language aspect of the summary exercises are given on page 82 of the Key.

Marking compositions

Exam compositions are not marked by examiners with perfect model answers next to them. They mark each script on its own merits and in accordance with an agreed interpretation of exam guidelines. (These are summarised in the table provided on page 83 of the Key.) When marking your own students' work, you can grade it appropriately and help them reach exam standards by using the following approach.

Firstly, a balanced view of a composition is important when you decide on an overall mark. One or two errors should not 'ruin' an effective piece of work if these are balanced out by other strengths. At IGCSE level, even the best students are expected to suffer from some frustration with the language and to make one or two mistakes, especially if they are being ambitious in their choice of grammar, vocabulary and idioms.

The best compositions, as a rule of thumb, are clear, straightforward and easy to read. They have definite beginnings and endings. The student shows involvement with the topic he/she is writing about, and is able to arouse your interest in it. Compositions of this kind can be given marks at the top end of the range.

Weak writing, on the other hand, is much more difficult to follow and you may find yourself re-reading it several times in order to make out the sense. As a reader, you don't feel drawn into the topic. After you have finished reading it, you may not be entirely clear about the meaning, or the student's opinions, or, if he/she was telling you a story, what exactly happened or how the story ended. Weak writing should be given marks at the lower end of the range.

Some writing is neither very good nor very weak. The task is interpreted in a safe but unexciting way. The meaning is clear but as a reader, you won't find it especially interesting or enjoyable to read. Average compositions of this type can be given middle-range marks.

Checklist for marking

In addition to the general guidance given above, you may like to use this checklist to help you when selecting a mark for your students' work.

1 *Answering the question*
  Does the writing cover the question set, or does it drift away from the question? If rubric prompts are given, are these addressed?

2 *Sentence construction*
  Do sentences begin and end in the right places? How varied are the sentences – are they a mixture of lengths or mostly short and simple? Are any relative clauses used?

3 *Grammar*

To what extent are tenses, modal verbs, conditionals and other grammatical features accurate where used? Is there some ambition in the use of grammatical structures, or does the student keep to very simple structures he/she can manage accurately?

4 *Vocabulary*

How varied and accurate is the vocabulary for the intended meaning? Does the student keep to limited and repetitive vocabulary, or is he/she making a real effort to use a wider range of vocabulary? Are any idioms used?

5 *Punctuation*

Is punctuation used? Is the punctuation accurate? Has the candidate set him/herself a more complex punctuation task (e.g. punctuating direct speech), and how well is this task achieved?

6 *Spelling*

How accurate is the spelling? Are simple, common words (e.g. *house*, *table*) spelled correctly? Are misspellings mostly because the student is trying to achieve a more ambitious effect with complex vocabulary? Are the spelling mistakes phonetic (e.g. *frend* for *friend*)? Remember, phonetic mistakes interfere less with communication than other kinds of spelling errors.

7 *Paragraphing*

Has the student organised his/her own work into paragraphs? Are the paragraphs in the right sequence and accurately linked together so the writing makes a coherent whole?

8 *Subject matter*

How well does the student deal with the topic? Does he/she get straight into the topic and seem interested in it, and also make the reader interested in it?

9 *Tone, register, sense of audience*

Do the tone, register and sense of audience feel right for the purpose? Competition entries, for example, should sound positive, enthusiastic and encouraging; a letter to a friend should sound friendly and sympathetic, whereas a letter to a newspaper should sound more formal and distanced.

10 *Sense of argument*

Is the argument set out clearly and logically and does the writer come to a clear conclusion? Are you sure what he/she thinks, or are there contradictions? Does the writer give clear examples? Are linking words (e.g. *however*, *moreover*) used, and do these help to make the meaning clear?

11 *Length of work*

Is the writing about the right length, within the word limit given?

Helping students improve their work

Setting and marking work is a tried and tested way of supporting learning. There are several ways of marking work so that students can learn and move on from their mistakes. Marking is most helpful when it is selective, so that some errors are highlighted and others are overlooked.

Error analysis

Error analysis is used to draw the attention of the class to an extract written by a fellow student which is a clear example of a mistake to avoid. You can read the extract aloud and ask students to analyse the error(s), or write the extract on the board. If your class is not familiar with error analysis, it is useful to explain the idea behind it so that the student who wrote the extract understands that the criticism is objective. Error analysis is a particularly useful way of giving feedback if you come across an example of something which has recently been taught to the class, e.g. an error in tone and register, or an inappropriate beginning or ending, or a point of grammar. It is best to focus the error analysis on a few sentences extracted from a student's composition, rather than looking at a whole piece of work.

Written feedback

In addition to error analysis, you can write comments at the end of students' work. The most helpful ones are usually specific comments that pick up on areas of language that have recently been taught. You can ask students to rewrite drafts of work to produce a better example. Misspelled words should be written out correctly for students to copy and learn. Areas of improvement should also be commented on and praised, to reinforce students' sense of progress and to continue to motivate and encourage.

ADVICE TO THE STUDENT

When facing an exam, many students naturally feel a little nervous. The information and advice below should help resolve your worries and enable you to do your best. Remember, lots of practice and hard work are the most important thing, so keep at it! You'll probably do much better than you think!

Paper 1, Reading and Writing (Core level)

The Core paper has seven exercises and must be completed in 90 minutes. There are two comprehension exercises, a form-filling exercise, a note-taking exercise with a linked summary exercise, and two composition questions. See the chart on pages 6/7 for more information.

Paper 2, Reading and Writing (Extended level)

The Extended paper has seven exercises and must be completed in two hours. There are two comprehension exercises (the second exercise may include finding a list of points), a form-filling exercise, a note-taking exercise, a summary exercise and two composition exercises. See the chart on pages 6/7 for more information.

Exercises 1 and 2 (Reading)

Exercise 1 is based on a brochure or advertisement with straightforward questions. Exercise 2 is based on a newspaper or magazine article and the information given in the text is more detailed. The way to do well in both exercises is to be as alert as possible to all the clues, to read quickly but with a lot of concentration, and to take care over the detail of the questions. For example, pictures/diagrams or headings supplied will give clues to meaning. Ask yourself: where is this text from and what is it likely to be about?

When reading, don't worry too much about words you don't understand – try to work them out from context. If you still don't understand, don't worry. Understanding them may not be necessary in order to give the right answer.

The questions often use different words and phrases to those given in the text because the exam is looking for understanding of meaning, not just matching words together. Find evidence for the answer by checking the text. Answer everything. You may get the answer right, even if you are not sure! The right answer to a question is one which contains the correct information, which can often be copied from the text. Answers can be very brief – a single word may be enough.

If you are asked a question such as *How much...?/How many...?/How long...?* requiring information about measurements, times, costs, percentages, etc, your answer must be specific. For example: *2 hours 10 minutes* (NOT *about 2 hours*), *The trip costs $149.50* (NOT *about $150*), *Five out of six houses* (NOT *Most houses*).

The questions usually follow the sequence of the text. For example, the answer to question (b) will be found at an earlier point in the text than the answer to question (c). Some questions have two bits to them. In this case, make sure you find answers to both bits of the question.

Exercise 2 may have a final question asking you to write a list of points. You can find the points by scanning the text and copying out the right information.

The number of marks allocated to each question is shown in brackets at the end of the question.

Exercise 3 (Form-filling)

This is an 'information transfer' exercise, which means you have to complete a form or set of notes based on information given. The key to doing really well in this exercise is to be careful with the detail and to check your work. You can get a lot of easy marks just by making sure facts such as names, addresses and telephone numbers are copied exactly. It's important that you spell everything correctly.

Exercise 4 (Note-taking)

Exercise 4 is not particularly hard because headings for the notes are given, and bullet points are supplied to guide your answers. Remember, each heading requires different bits of information from the text. Don't repeat anything you write or add any ideas or opinions of your own – everything has to come from the text. And remember that the finished notes should make sense! When practising, it's worth asking yourself: could someone reading these notes understand them even if they hadn't seen the original passage?

Exercise 5 (Summary)

In Exercise 5 you have to write a summary based on a text. In Paper 1, the summary exercise is linked to the notes for Exercise 4. All you need to do in this case is produce a clear paragraph in full sentences, reworking the notes you have already made and using some words of your own.

Extended candidates should read the text for their summary quickly and underline any relevant sections. Check back with the summary question. Join the ideas you have picked out into one or more coherent paragraphs, using some words and phrases of your own. Check back quickly again with the question and make any changes. Count the number of words. If you have time, make another draft of your summary, incorporating any changes. If you don't have time, simply make corrections to the first draft. In the exam itself, don't worry about the summary looking 'messy' as long as it is easily readable.

Make sure you read the question carefully because sometimes you are asked to include more than one aspect of the text in your summary.

Exercises 6 and 7 (Composition writing)

You need to do one task for each of these exercises. Typical tasks are writing a short formal or informal letter, or an article for the school magazine or a newspaper. In Exercise 7, prompts in the form of imaginary comments are usually given to help you understand the type of situation and to give you ideas. The key to starting well in the composition is to make sure you understand the situation, so give a little thought to what it's about before writing.

If you use the prompts in your composition, be selective (don't try to use them all), and expand them with reasons and examples. Don't just copy out the prompts, though – you won't get marks for copying. If you don't like the prompts, don't use them. You can write a good letter or article without any of them. Just check that your composition is still relevant to the question.

General advice on writing

The main point to remember is that the examiner is marking positively, looking for ways to reward you, not trying to criticise, so try to show the best you can do. One or two mistakes in grammar or spelling won't 'spoil' your work if the overall impression is good. Try to remember the following points:

- It's worth trying to **be a little ambitious** in your writing. Take one or two small risks to make your writing more interesting by using more complex structures or more unusual vocabulary. This can get a higher mark than sticking with safe but simple work.

- Let your personality shine through in your writing. The examiner will reward this. **Ideas and examples from your own life** are interesting to the examiner, even if you don't think so! Background details about your own life, family and school, and personal views which are relevant to the question, really help in gaining higher marks.

- **Plan before you write**. Think and plan in paragraphs. Three paragraphs are usually enough.

- **Keep to the point of the question, and cover all parts** – don't drift away and begin to write in general terms, and don't ignore any part of the question.

- **Take care** with grammar, spelling, vocabulary, punctuation and paragraphing. Indicate where paragraphs should be by putting // if you forget to write in paragraphs.

- **Proofread your work** at the end and correct careless mistakes.

- Have a **clear opening and closing sentence**. Examples:
  Formal letters
  I am interested in applying for...
  I was concerned to hear/read about...
  I look forward to hearing from you soon.
  I hope we will be able to arrange a meeting soon.
  Informal letters
  Just a quick line to tell you about Danielle's wedding.
  You'll be surprised when I tell you what happened to me last week!
  I must end now as I've got to catch up on my homework.
  It'll be great to see you next month. Give my love to everyone in the family.

- Use a **suitable tone and register**. For informal writing, instead of writing to an imaginary person such as Bill or Mary, it helps to think of someone you actually know (Ahmed? Pedro? Martina?) and to write to him or her. This will help to achieve a more natural tone and register.
  Sounding positive and enthusiastic makes a good impression and is the required tone for a competition entry. Balance negative ideas with positive points.

- Show **awareness of your audience** – a close friend, someone you haven't met before, a teenage magazine, a school newsletter, etc. Useful phrases for showing audience awareness are:
  I don't usually write to newspapers/the school magazine but I feel strongly about...
  My class has become involved in a really interesting project about...
  I think our school should...
  People of my age often feel...
  Do write back. I'd love to hear your views. (for the school magazine)
  I'd be very interested in hearing what other readers think. (for a newspaper)

Advice on time management

You'll probably find some exercises easy and others more challenging. Common sense in planning your time is your best aid. Core candidates have just under 13 minutes per exercise, but the exercises are not equal in difficulty and the marks given to them reflect this. Extended candidates have just over 17 minutes per exercise. Again, the exercises are not equally complex, so adjust the amount of time you spend, depending on how easy you find an exercise.

Think in minutes rather than parts of an hour – minutes do count and will add up. Keep a close eye on the clock. The longer you spend on one question, the less time you have for another. Don't spend too long on any one question – it's not worth it.

Don't count your words in the writing section. This is not necessary and, if you have practised, you will know what 150 or 200 words look like in your handwriting. Lined paper is provided in the exam as a guideline to the length required.

Exercise 1 is the 'easiest', but you don't have to start with the first exercise on the paper. Start wherever you feel comfortable and most confident. Don't forget about an exercise altogether, though!

This book will be very helpful because you can practise answering questions according to the time limit. Lots of practice really does make a big difference to speed and confidence. Be generous with yourself at first, then reduce the amount of time you allow yourself as your skills increase.

And finally...

We hope you enjoy using these Practice Tests, make lots of progress and achieve the success you are hoping for. Good luck!

CORE LEVEL

PRACTICE TEST 1

Exercise 1

Read the following advertisement about an unusual place to visit and then answer the questions on the opposite page.

THE DEEP

Visit **THE DEEP** and explore the great ocean floor from tropical coral lagoons to the icy wastes of Antarctica. Discover the story of the world's seas and oceans on a dramatic journey back in time and into the future.

This is Europe's deepest seawater aquarium containing 2.5 million litres of water and 87 tonnes of salt – home to the many fascinating seawater species you will see here.

AMAZING EXPERIENCES IN THE DEEP

- Ride in the world's only underwater glass elevator (lift), while surrounded by Sharks, Hog Fish, Moray Eels, and hundreds of other unusual and strange sea creatures.

- Drive a submarine in the futuristic research station, Deep Blue One, deep deep down on the ocean floor.

- Feel the ice-cold walls of the polar gallery section.

- Walk the ocean floor in Europe's deepest viewing tunnel while Sand Tiger Sharks and Leopard Sharks glide over your head.

- Watch the Sharks feeding – daily at 2 pm.

- See the magical jellyfish which 'disappears'.

- Be amazed at the huge prehistoric sea monsters pictured on our dramatic marine dinosaur wall.

OPENING TIMES
10 am to 6 pm daily (last ticket 5 pm).

HOW TO FIND US
Follow signs to Hull City Centre, then local signs for The Deep.
Watch out for the Hull Navigators in their distinctive yellow and red uniforms. They carry a wealth of knowledge and experience – all you need to do is ask.

VISITING THE CITY
Why not combine your visit to The Deep with a stroll along Hull's historic walkways, bursting with cafés, bars and restaurants? The Fish Pavement links directly to seven museums and the High Street shops. Hull's marina is a relaxing place to wander, full of yachts and cruise boats, and offering panoramic views across the River Humber.

(a) What exactly is The Deep?

.... [1]

(b) What is unusual about the underwater glass elevator?

.... [1]

(c) Apart from the glass elevator, how else can visitors observe life under the sea? Name **two** ways.

.... [1]

(d) Which feature of The Deep helps visitors learn about prehistoric sea monsters?

.... [1]

(e) What is the latest time a visitor can enter The Deep?

.... [1]

(f) Where in the city can you see yachts and cruise boats?

.... [1]

[Total: 6]

Exercise 2

The following newspaper article is about sugar cane, the plant which provides the world with sugar. Read it carefully and then answer the questions on the opposite page.

The tough grass that sweetens our lives

Sugar cane was once a wild grass that grew in New Guinea and was used by local people for roofing their houses and fencing their gardens. Gradually a different variety evolved which contained sucrose and was chewed on for its sweet taste. Over time, sugar cane became a highly valuable commercial plant, grown throughout the world. The majority of the world's sugar now comes from this particular commercial species.

Sugar became a vital ingredient in all kinds of things, from confectionery to medicine, and, as the demand for sugar grew, the industry became larger and more profitable. Unfortunately, however, the plant started to become weaker and more prone to disease. Many crops withered and died, despite growers' attempts to save them, and there were fears that the health of the plant would continue to deteriorate.

In the 1960s, scientists working in Barbados looked for ways to make the commercial species stronger and more able to resist disease. They experimented with breeding programmes, mixing genes from the wild species of sugar cane, which tends to be tougher, with genes from the more delicate, commercial type. Eventually, a commercial plant was developed which was 5 per cent sweeter than before, but also much stronger and less likely to die from disease. This sugar cane is not yet ready to be sold commercially, but when this happens, it is expected to be incredibly profitable for the industry.

Since the 1960s, scientists have been analysing the mysteries of the sugar cane's genetic code. Brazil, which produces one quarter of the world's sugar, has coordinated an international project under Professor Paulo Arrudo of the Universidade Estaudual de Campinas in São Paulo. Teams of experts have worked with him to discover more about which parts of the genetic structure of the plant are important for the production of sugar and its overall health.

Despite all the research, however, we still do not fully understand how the genes function in sugar cane. One major gene has been identified by Dr Angélique D'Hont and her team in Montpelier, France. This gene is particularly exciting because it makes the plant resistant to rust, a disease which probably originated in India, but is now capable of infecting sugar cane across the world. Scientists believe they will eventually be able to grow a plant which cannot be destroyed by rust.

Thanks to the pioneering work carried out by scientists in the last 50 years, sugar cane is now much more vigorous and the supply of sugar is therefore more guaranteed.

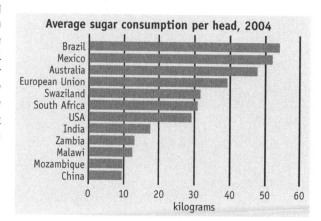

Average sugar consumption per head, 2004

(a) What were the original uses of wild sugar cane?

.... [1]

(b) Why did the demand for sugar increase?

.... [1]

(c) Why was the future of the sugar industry under threat? Give **two** reasons.

.... [1]

(d) How did the scientists working in Barbados produce a stronger commercial species of sugar cane?

.... [1]

(e) Why is the single gene identified by the scientists in France important for the health of the plant?

.... [1]

(f) Which countries consumed more than 40 kilos of sugar per person in 2004?

.... [1]

(g) Write **four** points to show why the future of the sugar industry looks positive, according to the article.

- ....

- ....

- ....

- .... [4]

[Total: 10]

Exercise 3

Lindy Melamu is 17 years old and lives at 984 Tembenko Road, Gaborone, Botswana. She is very interested in nature, and her favourite subjects at school are geography (she would love to travel more) and zoology. Along with other students at her school, she has been involved in voluntary work to transform an area of waste ground into a small farm which provides fresh vegetables and fruit for local people.

As part of the research she is doing for an ecology project, Lindy is learning about environmental projects around the world. On an internet website she sees an advertisement for a project in the Maldives which she would love to take part in. She would be particularly interested in a marine-based project to restore coral reefs.

Lindy is free after her exams finish, which is at the end of November, and her parents are willing to let her travel to the Maldives by herself, as long as she is back in time to help them with their busy season (starting in April) in the small hotel they run.

Lindy is a vegetarian and is in good health. Her telephone number is 267-3901278. She is also on email at melamu.l@remac.com.

ADVERTISEMENT

GLOBAL ECO-PROJECTS

As an international agency, **Global Eco-Projects** offers young people the chance to participate in some of today's most fascinating ecological projects. Although you will work as a volunteer and not be paid, the insights and experience you gain and the friendships you make will more than compensate.

This season we have a major new project in the fabulous **Maldives**, the breathtakingly-beautiful islands in the Indian Ocean. You can choose whether to be involved with the protection of endangered species or with environmental conservation (including tree-planting or safeguarding the fragile coral reefs). The programme also includes lectures on the development of the Maldives, and the opportunity to get to know the traditional way of life and sample the delicious cuisine.

If you are aged 16–30, don't hesitate to contact us today for more information.

Your planet needs you!

Imagine that you are Lindy and complete the form on the opposite page.

VOLUNTEER APPLICATION FORM / MALDIVES

(Please give your full name and address in CAPITAL LETTERS.)

NAME _____

ADDRESS _____

_____

TELEPHONE _____   EMAIL _____

Please circle your age group: 16–19   19–21   21–24   Over 24

Male / Female   (please delete)

How did you find out about Global Eco-Projects?

_____

Are you intending to travel alone?   Yes / No   (please delete)

If you have a preference for any particular project, please specify:

_____

Please specify any special dietary requirements: _____

Do you have any medical conditions the organisers should be aware of? _____

Which time(s) of the year are you available?_____

In the space below, please write **one sentence** giving information about any experience you have of environmental work, and **one sentence** explaining what you hope to gain from the project.

_____

_____

_____

[Total: 10]

Exercise 4

Read the newspaper article below about dolphins and their relationship with man. Then complete the note-taking exercise which follows.

OUR TRUE FRIEND THE DOLPHIN

The dog may be 'man's best friend' but the sharp-eyed dolphin, with its cheery smile and intuitive intelligence, is the creature we love to love. Whether it's delighting whale-watchers or swimming playfully with scuba divers, the dolphin's ability to delight the world of humans has made it one of our favourites in the animal kingdom.

'Like us, dolphins are great communicators,' says Jo Clark, Conservation Officer for the Whale and Dolphin Conservation Society. They are very social, and communicate through a range of clicks, whistles and calls. Researchers say that each dolphin has its own unique whistle, which may identify it to others.'

Dolphins live in groups and work together to feed and to drive away predators. Orcas, a kind of dolphin known more commonly as killer whales, have strong family bonds and remain together in family groups called pods, which have their own individual language dialect. They are known to pass down knowledge from one generation to the next. Scientists are now suggesting that the only equivalent to the complex and stable relationships in orca groups is found in human societies.

Jo says, 'There are many examples of dolphins forming partnerships with people. For three generations, in Laguna, Brazil, a group of bottlenosed dolphins have been working with fishermen to catch mullet. The dolphins drive the fish towards the fishermen's nets, even signalling with a splash of their tails when the nets should be thrown.'

A particularly dramatic account of dolphins protecting humans from danger was reported by a group of fishermen from South Carolina in the United States in 2001. Their boat sank 50 kilometres from the shore and they found themselves surrounded by mako, hammerhead and tiger sharks. A group of dolphins arrived and set about driving the sharks away. They remained all night and the following day, protecting the fishermen from any sharks that came near.

Witnesses have also seen dolphins saving people from drowning, when there was no apparent benefit to themselves. We'll never know for certain why dolphins act like this at times. What we do know is that they have to protect their families from attacks by sharks, so it is possible they are acting instinctively when they help people or that they extend their concept of family to include an obviously vulnerable human.

But while dolphins display such loyal feelings towards man, the compassion is unfortunately often one way. Pollution and being drowned in fishing nets are two of the terrible dangers they face from us. Up to 10,000 dolphins and their cousins the porpoises are killed in the North Atlantic each year as a result of the fishing industry. Their habitats are destroyed and they are bombarded by noise. We even capture them and keep them in tanks, in spite of seeing what rich lives these wonderfully intelligent creatures lead in the wild.

You are planning to give a short talk to a wildlife club about people and dolphins.

On the notepad opposite, make **two** short notes under each heading as a plan for your talk. Do not use complete sentences. An example is given under the first heading

PEOPLE AND DOLPHINS

Similarities between people and dolphins

- *family structure / live as part of a group*

- .... [1]

- .... [1]

Practical ways dolphins have helped people

- .... [1]

- .... [1]

How people threaten their survival

- .... [1]

- .... [1]

[Total: 6]

Exercise 5

Imagine that you have given your talk to the wildlife club. Now you want to make a summary of your talk, to be published on a wildlife internet site.

Look at your notes in Exercise 4 above. Using the ideas in your notes, write a summary describing the ways dolphins and people are similar, and what is known about their impact on each other.

Your summary should be one paragraph of no more than 70 words. You should use your own words as far as possible.

....

....

....

....

....

....

[Total: 4]

Exercise 6

STARTING NEXT MONTH!!!

YOUR

NEW ...   VIBRANT ...

EXCITING ... TOPICAL ...

COLLEGE MAGAZINE

Are you young and full of fun?

Do you have strong views and ideas?

Do you want to have a say in what happens at college?

Can you write well in English?

Then you can help – we need you to join us as a regular writer!

Write now to the Editor and tell us why you are suitable.

You have seen a poster at your college about a new magazine and would like to be involved. **Write a letter offering to be a writer for the magazine. Your letter should be about 100–150 words long.**

Don't forget to include:

- details about yourself and why you are suitable

- why you want to write for the magazine

- what kinds of articles you could contribute.

You will receive up to 5 marks for the content of your letter, and up to 5 marks for the style and accuracy of your language.

....

....

....

....

....

....

....

....

....

....

....

....

....

....

....

....

....

....

....

....

....

....

.... [10]

....

Exercise 7

Your school wishes to send a sports team overseas to take part in a special international sports event for schools. Here are some comments about this idea from people in your class:

'How exciting! We'll be able to learn about a different culture and make new friends.'

'I don't like the idea – the competitions will be even more stressful than usual.'

'I'd love to go! Sport is a way to create peace and harmony between people.'

'I don't mind – as long as it doesn't distract us from our exam preparation.'

Write an article for your school magazine giving your views about the issue. Your article should be about 100–150 words long.

The comments above may give you some ideas, but you are free to use any ideas of your own.

You will receive up to 5 marks for the content of your article, and up to 5 marks for the style and accuracy of your language.

....

....

....

....

....

....

....

....

....

....

....

....

....

....

....

....

....

....

....

....

.... [10]

....

EXTENDED LEVEL

PRACTICE TEST 2

Exercise 1

Read the following advertisement for the Euro Space Center, and then answer the questions on the opposite page.

Come and take a space walk –

in a new dimension!

Reach for the stars at the unique **Euro Space Center**. Find out everything you need to know about space – from the origins of the universe to the most futuristic space exploration plans. Light, sound and special effects help to bring your space journey to life. Throughout your tour, our specially trained guides will answer your questions and provide you with any information you require.

Begin your tour with our interactive exhibition about the planets, then move on to the **Space Laboratory** and see some of the experiments carried out in space. Visit our international space station, where you can climb into our full-scale **Space Shuttle** model and experience life on board as an astronaut.

You will know all about space by now and, to help you further, our Space Center astronaut will tell you about how young people train as astronauts in our own training school. Finally, you can watch our amazing **Space Show** in our IMAX cinema. Sponsored by the Space Foundation, this dynamic show will reinforce everything you have learned during your visit.

Outside we have an extensive car and coach park (no charge), and an outdoor exhibition including a giant solar system, full-size rocket models, a space labyrinth, a huge sundial and outdoor games. Don't worry if it rains – much of this is under cover.

After that, why not visit our restaurant **Resto Space** for food and drink on a space theme? And don't forget our **Space Shop**, offering you a huge range of souvenirs and gifts to take home.

The Euro Space Center is open every day during school holidays, and additionally from Easter to 1st November except Mondays. Opening times are 10.00–5.00.

For entrance fees and group admission rates, call our **booking service** on +32-61-650133. Or you can email us for up-to-date entry information at info@eurospacecenter.be.

Euro Space Center
B-6890 Transinne
Belgium

(a) How does the Space Center make space seem real to the visitor?

.... [1]

(b) How can you find out extra information during your visit?

.... [1]

(c) What can you learn about in the Space Laboratory?

.... [1]

(d) How can you find out what it feels like to be an astronaut?

.... [1]

(e) What is the purpose of the cinema show?

.... [1]

(f) How is it possible to visit the outside items if the weather is bad?

.... [1]

(g) On which days in October is the Space Center closed?

.... [1]

(h) Exactly how can you find out about admission fees, apart from sending an email?

.... [1]

[Total: 8]

Exercise 2

Read the following magazine article about beekeeping in Zambia and then answer the questions on the opposite page.

Hive Aid

It is 4.45 a.m. in Samasati village in north-western Zambia and the Chimwanga family, champion beekeepers, are already on their way to extract honey from one of their many hives. For as long as anyone can remember, this area has been famous for beekeeping, but it is only in the last ten years that the business has begun to make a difference to the lives of the producers, since they began to trade through an organisation guaranteeing them a fair price for their crop.

Samasati is a beautiful place, where nature provides and pollution is non-existent. Here, 60 miles from the nearest telephone or source of electricity, the 300 inhabitants support themselves from the forest and rivers. Life is hard, however, and the only income available to the villagers is from selling their honey. The Chimwangas own a small house and a couple of bicycles and are the village's biggest honey producers. When his children are old enough, Mr Chimwanga should be able to send them to school and will be able to pay for medical care if any of his family becomes ill. The Chimwangas are proud that the head of their family is the best beekeeper in the village.

It is a half-hour walk from the Chimwanga house to the hive. The hives themselves are made out of cylindrical sections of tree bark, which are hung high up in the trees to attract swarms of bees. (The tree eventually regrows its bark, so there is a never-ending supply for new hives.) Bee hives in Zambia have been made in this way for thousands of years. On reaching the site, the Chimwangas tear off low, leaf-covered branches from

nearby trees. They place these in a pile on the ground as a bundle and insert some dry reed stalks in the middle. A match then sets the reeds alight and thick smoke is produced as the fire spreads from the dry reeds to the green leaves.

Mr Chimwanga climbs nimbly up the tree trunk and moves carefully along a branch towards the hanging hive. He carries the smoking bundle on a length of string tied around his waist. When he reaches the hive, he waves smoke into the entrance to calm the bees and then thrusts his arm inside. The bees circle his head and hum relentlessly. Unafraid, he pulls up a bucket and fills it with the precious honeycomb, dropping some pieces down to his family to eat as he does so. It is the most delicious honey, fragrant but not too sweet – the result of the hundreds of orchids and other wild flowers the bees have feasted on in the forest.

This honey is sold straight to the exporting company, North West Bee Products, through their buyer, Bob Malichi. He is the vital middleman for the beekeepers and arrives in the village amid claps and warm handshakes, weighs the honey and pays the producers directly.

Bob himself comes from generations of beekeepers and is passionate about Zambian honey – indeed, he believes it is Zambia's future. 'Honey will always be there,' he says. 'If you look after the bees, they will produce for you. Our honey is organically produced. There's no pollution, and nothing is added – it comes straight from the forest.' The honey is transported to Dar es Salaam, in neighbouring Tanzania, for export. Within a month of a Zambian beekeeper climbing to his hive, his honey can be spread on bread anywhere in the world.

(a) Why has the honey trade recently become profitable for Zambian beekeepers?

.... [1]

(b) How do we know Samasati is a remote, isolated village?

.... [1]

(c) How do the villagers provide for themselves?

.... [1]

(d) Which two items show Mr Chimwanga's status as a successful beekeeper?

.... [1]

(e) How can Mr Chimwanga's income benefit his children?

.... [1]

(f) Explain how a Zambian beehive is made.

.... [1]

(g) What gives Zambian honey its characteristic taste?

.... [1]

(h) How does the reader know that the whole process from hive to table is quick?

.... [1]

(i) Make a list of **six** points explaining how Zambian beekeepers gather and sell their honey crop.

- ....

- ....

- ....

- ....

- ....

- .... [6]

[Total: 14]

Exercise 3

Jeanne Lavale is an 18-year-old student at the Art Deco College of Art and Design in Antwerp, Belgium. She is hoping to be chosen as 'Antwerp Artist of the Year' with her paintings and sculptures which she began two years ago at the age of sixteen, when she started at the college. She has been painting and sculpting since she was eight years old.

To enter the 'Antwerp Artist of the Year' competition, she has to present two paintings and one three-dimensional piece. While studying at the college she has completed twenty paintings using various media – oils, watercolours, acrylics and pen-and-ink. She has also produced a collection of wood and metal sculptures representing changes in the technical world over the last fifty years. Although her favourite sculpture is called 'Space Rocket', she feels that this is not the one to choose for the competition, so she has decided to send in 'Machine Mind' instead.

Her paintings for the competition, both watercolours, will be from her collection 'Friends', and she has chosen 'Julie', a portrait of her best friend Julie Vasey. Her second choice is a view of Herentals, the town where she grew up. It is called simply 'Home'.

If she wins the competition she will get an opportunity for her paintings or sculpture to be shown in galleries all over Europe. There is also a cash prize of 2000 euros. This would help her to continue working as an artist after leaving college, and also to fulfil her ambition to start a painting workshop for children aged 5 to 7.

The competition rules require the paintings and sculpture to be ready for collection on either 17th or 19th July, and the organisers will contact the college to agree a convenient time. Jeanne needs to give the name of her art teacher, Mrs V. Bernet, whose contact telephone number is 571-9300, extension 403. The college is at 27 Tervurenlaan in Antwerp. Alternatively, entrants may, if they prefer, deliver their own artworks to the organisers during the weekend of 14th and 15th July. In this case, they should go to the Kattenberg Studio at 5 Avenue Boitsfort, Antwerp, between 10 a.m. and 4 p.m. on either day. After consulting Mrs Bernet, Jeanne has decided to ask for her artworks to be collected from the college on the first of the two possible dates.

Imagine you are Jeanne, and complete the application form on the opposite page, using the information above.

ANTWERP ARTIST OF THE YEAR

Please complete all of **Part A** *in CAPITALS.*

PART A

Name of artist ....

Age ....

Number of years of formal art study ....

School/College attended ....

Address ....

PART B

Media/materials used for competition artworks. *Please circle as many as required*:

Oils   Acrylics   Watercolours   Charcoal   Clay   Stone   Metal   Wood   Plastic   Other (*Please specify*) ....

I wish to enter the following
artworks for the competition: Name of Painting 1   ....

Name of Painting 2   ....

Name of Sculpture   ....

PART C

Complete as appropriate: I wish to   (a) have my artworks collected on .... July.

or   (b) deliver them to the Kattenberg Studio on .... July.

If you have chosen (a), please provide: College contact number ....

Name of member of staff ....

PART D

In no more than 20 words, use the box below to tell us how you would use the prize money.

[Total: 8]

Exercise 4

Read the following article about watercress, a vitamin-rich salad vegetable. Then complete the notes on the opposite page.

Watercress

Crisp, green and peppery, watercress is positively packed with healthy vitamins and minerals. It has a long history: the Greek god Zeus was reputed to think that watercress helped in building health and strength, while Hippocrates, 'the father of medicine', was so convinced that watercress was a great healer that he built his first hospital next to a stream so that he could grow a plentiful supply of the glossy green leaves for his patients. The Romans chewed watercress in large quantities, believing that it would cure baldness. Modern-day celebrities recommend a watercress-soup diet as a great way to lose weight healthily.

Watercress sandwiches were traditionally a breakfast item in nineteenth-century Europe. A nickname for watercress, in fact, was 'poor man's bread', because it was often eaten on its own for breakfast by families which could not afford the bread to go with it.

Watercress is a member of the mustard family and, as its name suggests, it is grown in water – in warm, shallow streams of flowing spring water. It contains vitamins C (66mg per 100g), K and A, and is also a valuable source of iron, potassium, copper and calcium. Like broccoli and spinach, it has special properties which help prevent cancer. The mustard oils in its glossy leaves and stems contain a chemical compound known as PEITC. Recent research has proved that this compound can inhibit the growth of cancer cells and, in some cases, actually destroy them.

The best watercress has silky green leaves without any marks and crisp, undamaged stems. The older the plant, the darker are its leaves and the thicker its stems. This means a higher concentration of oils and vitamins. Young watercress, on the other hand, may be harvested after only 28 days growth and has a milder flavour. It is best to eat watercress fresh and raw, to preserve more of its valuable nutrients, but it can be lightly cooked and used as an alternative to spinach – another dark green vegetable – in various recipes. From soups to salads to stir-fries, watercress is now acclaimed around the world as a natural, healthy superfood.

You are going to give a short talk about watercress to your class. Complete the notes below as a basis for your talk. Some of the notes have been completed for you.

(a) Examples of the use of watercress through the ages:

- *Zeus thought watercress was good for health and strength.*

- *Hippocrates grew watercress by his hospital to heal the patients.*

- *Romans* .... [1]

- .... [1]

- .... [1]

(b) Health-giving properties of watercress:

- .... [1]

- .... [1]

- *Contains cancer-preventing PEITC.*

(c) Buying and eating watercress:

- the best: .... [1]

- older watercress: .... [1]

- young watercress: .... [1]

- *eat it raw or cooked.*

[Total: 8]

Exercise 5

Read the following article about trade and then write a summary of its history.

Your summary should be about 100 words. You should use your own words as far as possible.

You will receive up to 6 marks for the content of your summary, and up to 4 marks for the style and accuracy of your language.

Born to TRADE

It is sometimes thought that the longing for material goods, the need to buy things, is a relatively modern invention, but in fact its roots go back to the dawn of humanity. Trade or 'shopping' is certainly an ancient obsession, and existed before our ancestors invented writing, laws, cities or farming, even before they used metal to make tools.

Humans are born to trade; and we don't need shops or money to do it. Evidence from modern hunter-gatherers suggests that the exchange of food and other essentials comes naturally, as well as the ability to keep a record of the credits and debits involved. And once trade begins, the economic benefits are hard to resist.

Until less than fifty years ago, a group of coastal aboriginals in northern Australia traded fish hooks, along a chain of trading partners, with people living 400 miles inland, who cut and polished local stone to make axes. Every individual along the chain made a profit, in the form of hooks or axes, even if he produced neither himself. And both groups of 'manufacturers', by concentrating on things they could produce efficiently and exchanging them for other things they needed, benefited as a result.

Trade in the necessities of life, such as food and simple tools, is not really surprising, considering the link between these basic items and survival. What is surprising, though, is that our taste for luxury items – objects with no obvious survival value – also goes back a long way. Archaeologists used to think that 'consumer culture' first began about 40,000 years ago. However, recent findings in Africa, of art, jewellery, cosmetics and decorative objects, are pushing the origins of consumerism much further back into human 'prehistory'.

In South Africa, 100,000-year-old decorative dyes have been found in a region where none were produced; it is thought that these goods had been bought at least 30 kilometres away. Beads 76,000 years old were also found at the same site. These earliest beads known to us were not just random findings – they were grouped together in size and had holes like those used for threading onto a necklace.

Archaeologists argue that trade prepared the way for the complex societies in which we live today. Modern-day shoppers may not be impressed by simple beads, axes and fishing hooks, but their modern equivalents – fast cars and designer labels – hold the same fascination for us as 'trade goods' did for people 100,000 years ago.

[10]

Exercise 6

There are plans to close down your local railway line at the end of the year because of financial difficulties. This line connects with the main line to your capital city in one direction, and with a ferry to a nearby island in the other direction. It is also vital for transporting students to your college, as the train runs every 30 minutes whereas the local bus service is very infrequent.

Write a letter to the editor of your local newspaper, giving your views about this situation. **Your letter should be about 150–200 words long**.

Don't forget to include:

- how this issue affects you and your family and friends

- how your town will be affected

- any alternative suggestions you can make.

You will receive up to 9 marks for the content of your letter, and up to 9 marks for the style and accuracy of your language.

....

....

....

....

....

....

....

....

....

....

....

....

....

....

....

....

....

....

....

....

....

....

.... [18]

....

Exercise 7

Some people think it is important to have at least one very good teacher while you are at school or college, but not everyone agrees. Here are some comments from people you have discussed this with:

'I'll always be grateful to Mrs Owen, who made maths so simple for me.'

'If I hadn't had a sympathetic teacher when I changed schools I would never have passed any exams.'

'My business is a direct result of the suggestions of my IT teacher.'

'I never liked any of my teachers and they didn't like me. It hasn't done me any harm.'

'I think my friends have had most influence on me at school.'

'My parents were always the people who encouraged me most.'

Write an article for your college magazine, giving your views on this topic. Your article should be about 150–200 words long.

The comments above may give you some ideas, but you are free to use ideas of your own.

You will receive up to 9 marks for the content of your article, and up to 9 marks for the style and accuracy of your language.

....

....

....

....

....

....

....

....

....

....

....

....

....

....

....

....

....

....

....

....

....

....

....

....

....

....

....

....

.... [18]

....

PRACTICE TEST 3

Exercise 1

Read the following information about Seychelles and then answer the questions on the opposite page.

The Republic of Seychelles is a group of 115 islands of truly striking beauty, lying in the Indian Ocean 1800 km east of Kenya. Popular with tourists, Seychelles is also a natural sanctuary for an amazing diversity of bird and animal life, such as the world's smallest frog, the heaviest land tortoise and the only flightless bird of the Indian Ocean.

Culture and cuisine

The Seychellois, numbering around 80,000 people, are a colourful and harmonious blend of different races. People from almost every race on earth have at one time or another contributed something of their own customs and cultures to the islands. This diversity is clearly reflected in Seychellois cooking. From Asian influences come delicious stir fries and fiery curries, while the European influence, especially French, is apparent in the use of herbs and garlic. Some of the best fish in the world can be found here – the popular red snapper or 'bourzwa' is a favourite with both locals and tourists.

Environment

Unique plants and animals have evolved in Seychelles to produce some of the rarest examples of flora and fauna in the world. Seychelles also boasts two World Heritage Sites: Aldabra Atoll and the Vallee de Mai, where the magnificent coco de mer palm grows. The government has declared 46% of the total land mass (452 sq km) as national parks, nature reserves or protected areas. A further 228 sq km have been designated as Marine National Park to safeguard marine creatures and habitat. As land is scarce, waste disposal can be a problem. Where possible, therefore, rubbish such as toothpaste cartons and empty shampoo bottles should be taken back to the visitor's country of origin.

Weather

Seychelles enjoys a pleasant tropical climate with an average humidity of 75%. The islands lie outside the cyclone belt and there are no extremes of weather. When the south-east trade winds blow between May and September, there is generally less rainfall, but rougher seas. The north-west trade winds, which blow from November to March, bring the wet season. From March to May and September to November, the seas are calmest, with the best visibility and conditions.

Average max. temp. °C

Jan	Feb	Mar	Apr	May	Jun	Jul	Aug	Sep	Oct
30	30	31	31	30	29	29	28	29	29

Nov	Dec
30	30

Average monthly rainfall (mm)

Jan	Feb	Mar	Apr	May	Jun	Jul	Aug	Sep	Oct
379	271	169	178	101	51	63	101	117	210

Nov	Dec
217	283

Regulations for tourists

For immigration clearance, tourists need a valid passport, a return or onward ticket, proof of accommodation, and sufficient funds for the duration of their stay. A valid yellow fever vaccination certificate is also required from travellers who have recently come from an infected area.

a) What unique specimens of wildlife can be found on the islands? Give **two** examples.

.... [1]

b) Why is the food eaten in Seychelles so varied?

.... [1]

c) What action has been taken to protect sea life?

.... [1]

d) What are visitors asked to do to avoid pollution on the islands?

.... [1]

e) What is the main influence on the climate?

.... [1]

f) What are good times of the year for visitors interested in diving and other water sports?

.... [1]

g) Which are the two driest months of the year in Seychelles?

.... [1]

h) What evidence is required to prove that visitors from certain areas are not infected by disease?

.... [1]

[Total: 8]

Exercise 2

Read the following article about elephants in Kenya and then answer the questions on the opposite page.

IN KENYA'S AMBOSELI NATIONAL PARK

a wise old elephant keeps watch over her large family. The African Elephant Conservation Trust has named this gentle matriarch Echo and has followed her life for more than 30 years. Echo is sensitive and caring when with her family, but becomes fearless when threatened by animal or man. Her leadership qualities are admirable as she guides her family through danger.

When Echo was first found and studied by the Conservation Trust, she was 23 years old. Having just survived the deaths of the more senior members of the herd, she had adopted a motherly role for seven of her family. Now she is nearly 60. Once, when her 10-day-old calf was kidnapped by other elephants, Echo encouraged three adult females from her own herd to help her to track and attack the enemy and successfully rescue the baby. Poachers, hunters, famine and drought have all taken their toll on Echo's extended family yet, thanks to her successful leadership through many difficulties, the herd has now grown to 27 members of all ages.

Meanwhile, Echo has become world famous, thanks to three films about her life and behaviour, by award-winning film-maker Martyn Colbeck. His work has changed public perception of elephants by demonstrating the high level of intelligence and social behaviour of these complex creatures. The respect and interest generated by the films have helped to save this species, which at one time was threatened with extinction. Recent research by the Conservation Trust has also revealed valuable information about birth and death rates and the fact that elephants

communicate at a very sophisticated level. They celebrate birth, have lifelong friendships and even mourn the death of family members.

The elephant population in Kenya fell from 130,000 in 1973 to less than 20,000 in 1989, a loss of 85%. The reason for this disastrous decline was, of course, mankind – mainly because elephants were hunted intensively for their ivory tusks. Destruction of habitat made the problem worse.

It is not all bad news for African elephants, however. In the Amboseli National Park they have been increasing steadily in numbers. In this protected area of 150 square miles in southern Kenya, they can live relatively undisturbed in a natural habitat – because the presence of researchers and tourists has kept poachers away and, equally importantly, the local Masai people have supported the project. Unlike other places in Africa, where hunting and poaching still take place, here the elephant family structure is being preserved and the population spans the whole range from newborn calves to adults as old as Echo.

To find out more about the work of the African Elephant Conservation Trust and to follow news about Echo and her family, simply visit the website at www.elephanttrust.org.

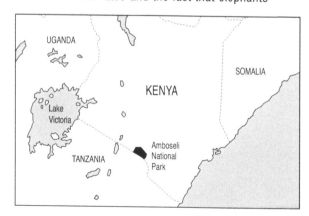

This article first appeared in the January 2005 issue of Saga magazine.

(a) What is the name of the research organisation featured in the article?

.... [1]

(b) How does the article describe the temperament of Echo? Give **three** of her qualities.

.... [1]

(c) Describe an example of Echo's skill in managing difficult situations.

.... [1]

(d) What **two** natural events threatened Echo's family?

.... [1]

(e) Name **two** human activities which are to blame for the decline of the African elephant, according to the article.

.... [1]

(f) How do the Maasai people feel about the protection given to the elephants?

.... [1]

(g) What impact has the protection provided by the National Park had on the elephants' family groups?

.... [1]

(h) Name **two** types of information provided by the website.

.... [1]

(i) According to the article, what new knowledge about African elephants has the research given us? List **six** points.

- ....

- ....

- ....

- ....

- ....

- ....[6]

[Total: 14]

Exercise 3

Chen Lee is sixteen years old and attends Oakton High School. He has lived at 21 Orange Tree Avenue, Oakton since he was ten years old, when his father got a job with a boatbuilding factory in the town. Before moving to Oakton, Chen lived at 19 Jubilee Road, Kingsby, a nearby city. The family have never regretted the move and have learned to enjoy the peace and tranquillity of the smaller town.

Chen likes the friendliness of the people, and the fact that most of his friends live nearby. As well as being a safe area, without much crime, Oakton is a very attractive place with a riverside walk. It also has several small natural conservation areas, but Chen wishes there were more of these.

Oakton is a quiet town with only 30,000 people and 8,000 homes. It has a swimming pool which Chen visits every Saturday with his friends, and they usually drop in for a snack at Ellie's Café afterwards. Apart from swimming once a week, he attends a video/DVD club at the local Community Centre (Chen is very interested in films), although he has to go to a cinema complex in Kingsby to see the latest releases. He enjoys sport and plays tennis or football in the park most weeks with his friends.

There is a small row of shops in Oakton: a greengrocer's, a supermarket, a general store/post office and a bakery. Chen uses the general store/post office on a regular basis to buy stamps (he has many pen friends) or sweets and soft drinks, and he buys things at the other shops occasionally. He thinks the shopping facilities are satisfactory but wishes he could buy CDs or shoes without having to go to Kingsby, 30 kilometres away.

Oakton has a popular and well-established Good Neighbour Scheme which aims to help people in the community who need assistance with everyday tasks. Chen's father visits an elderly neighbour once a fortnight and tidies her garden, takes out her rubbish and does little repair jobs. Chen usually helps too, and takes over if his father is too busy with work to do extra chores. Neither of them takes any payment for this.

Various improvements have been made in Oakton over recent years. Street lighting is more extensive and there is a more frequent bus service with improved connections. In addition, after complaints about litter and issues of hygiene, there are now more frequent rubbish collections. A recycling bank for glass bottles and tins has proved very popular, and the facility is due to be expanded to include plastic containers very shortly. Road safety in Oakton was a cause for concern until road safety cameras were installed on the main roads; this has reduced the number of speeding drivers.

Opportunities for young people improved when the Community Centre was extended, but Chen thinks more could be offered to the 14–18 age group, who would enjoy a room set aside at the Community Centre especially for them. Some residents feel the building of new houses should be restricted, but Chen and most of his friends believe extra housing is needed to provide for young people, who currently leave Oakton to look for accommodation and work.

The government is carrying out a survey on selected towns in the area. Imagine you are Chen Lee and complete the survey form opposite.

LOCAL TOWNS FACT-FINDING SURVEY

Please help us to find out more about the opinions of residents in local towns by completing this survey form.

SECTION 1

Please write your name and address in block capitals.

Name: _____

Address : _____

Age: _____ Occupation: _____

Approximately how long have you lived in the town? _____

If you have lived in the town for less than three years, please write your previous address:

_____

Approximate population of your town. (*Please circle.*)

    Under 12000   12000–15000   15000–25000   25000–40000   More than 40000

Approximate number of homes. (*Please delete numbers not applicable.*)

    Fewer than 3000   3000–6000   6000–12000   12000–24000   More than 24000

How did you come to live in the town? (*Please tick.*)

❏ Born here   ❏ Came with family   ❏ Other
❏ Got employment in area   ❏ Marriage
❏ Retired here   ❏ Attracted by peacefulness of area

Which of the following facilities in your town do you use on a regular basis? (Please tick.)

❏ Sports Centre   ❏ Swimming Pool   ❏ Cafés/Restaurants
❏ Cinema   ❏ Recreation Ground/Park   ❏ Clubs

Do you do any voluntary work in the town?   Yes / No (*Please circle.*)

If Yes, give details: _____

From the following list, tick **three** items that are most important to you for future development in your town.

❏ More extensive recycling facilities   ❏ More nature conservation areas   ❏ Better choice of shops
❏ Improved transport connections   ❏ Wider use of road safety cameras
❏ Facilities for teenagers   ❏ Restriction on the building of new houses

SECTION 2

The government wishes to increase industrial development and needs to identify suitable places for this in the local region. Write one sentence of **12–20 words** saying how you would feel about more industrial development in your town.

_____

_____

[Total: 8]

Exercise 4

Read the following article from a sports magazine about dehydration during exercise. Then complete the notes on the opposite page.

Time To Get Drinking!

Did you know that sixty per cent of your body weight is water? If you weigh 70 kilos, for example, you are carrying 42 kilos of water around with you! However, a loss of only two per cent of this water through dehydration during exercise can significantly affect your performance. The more you sweat, the more your exercise performance declines, unless you drink enough to replace your loss of fluids.

When you lose too much water, you can overheat quite easily, especially in a warm environment. But this is not the only problem you may face. Dehydration leads to your heart pumping much faster, which means exercise becomes more difficult and requires more effort. Despite these problems, however, many of us simply do not take enough fluids when we head for the gym or set out on a run.

So why is this? How do we manage to lose so much water without simply drinking more to replace it? Well, it's easier than you think. When we are at rest, we quickly become aware that we are thirsty and will put that right by having a drink. When we exercise,

on the other hand, our thirst mechanism does not work as efficiently, so we don't notice early enough that we are actually thirsty. In fact, we only start to feel thirsty when we have already lost around two per cent of our body weight (the point at which our performance is affected).

Another problem is that, the more dehydrated we become during exercise, the more difficult it is to prevent further dehydration – because our stomachs become intolerant to fluids and we do not absorb water properly, just when we need it most.

The key thing about fluids and exercise is to manage your intake properly – regular small amounts are preferable, and some should be drunk before the period of exercise begins. You also need to match your intake to the sort of exercise you are doing. For example, for one hour of exercise, such as taking part in a 10 km run, you need to drink about two extra litres of water. For longer periods of exercise, sports drinks containing carbohydrate are recommended.

You are preparing to give a short talk to your class about dehydration during exercise. Make short notes for your talk under the following headings. Two of the notes have been done for you.

Effects of dehydration during exercise

- *Performance declines*

- .... [1]

- .... [1]

- .... [1]

Why we may not get enough fluids during exercise

- .... [1]

- .... [1]

How to avoid dehydration during exercise

- .... [1]

- .... [1]

- .... [1]

- *Drink sports drinks containing carbohydrate for longer periods of exercise.*

[Total: 8]

Exercise 5

Read the following article about perfume and then write a summary explaining why perfume manufacturers use artificial ingredients.

Your summary should be about 100 words. You should use your own words as far as possible.

You will receive up to 6 marks for the content of your summary, and up to 4 marks for the style and accuracy of your language.

Perfume

The use of scent dates back to earliest times. The ancient Egyptians perfumed the bricks used to build their houses and temples, and wore cones of perfumed fat in their hair. Fragrant cedar wood was thought to preserve bodies, and temple doors were made from it. We know that perfume was used in ancient purification rituals, and that the Romans used lavender in their baths.

These days, consumer demand for perfumed products is intense. In the home, from detergents to paper tissues, soap to shoe polish, fragrance is the common ingredient. Artificial leather is perfumed to make it smell like the real thing, and on the New York subway the scent of camomile has been tested as an anti-crime aid. In Japan, some companies spray scent through the building's air-conditioning system at key times of the working day.

To meet the demands of the perfume industry, manufacturers use ingredients from many countries: rose from Morocco, eucalyptus from Portugal, patchouli from Indonesia and sandalwood from India. Scientific developments also mean that companies can use substitutes for some natural ingredients.

Scientists have discovered that natural and synthetic materials are highly complementary and are acceptable to the consumer. Even the most expensive perfumes are in fact compounds of both natural and synthetic ingredients. The French perfume manufacturers were among the first to incorporate synthetics when they made the famous perfume *Chanel No 5* in 1923. Coty's *L'Aimant* and Lanvin's *Arpège* followed in 1927.

Producing natural oils is very expensive. For example, 1000 kilos of jasmine flowers make just one kilo of extract. Using synthetic fragrance has reduced the costs of manufacture overall, although the chemical operations involved can be very time-consuming and costly – sixteen or seventeen chemical separations may be needed to produce the right result. Nevertheless, the use of sophisticated chemicals to reproduce fragrances is likely to increase, as the supply of many natural ingredients is insufficient to meet demand. Nature's own products are subject to variations in the weather, pests, changes in natural oil yield and crop failure. Using artificial ingredients as well as natural oils gives perfume manufacturers more control over the production process, which is why many classic perfumes owe their characteristic top notes to the fruits of science, not nature.

Ingredients, whether natural or synthetic, are not the main cost of a fragrance, however. Packaging, marketing and advertising make up a higher percentage of the final cost.

....

....

....

....

....

....

....

....

....

....

....

....

....

....

....

....

....

....

....

.... [10]

....

Exercise 6

ANIMAL LIFE MAGAZINE

COMPETITION

Write and tell us about an animal or bird that you like and admire.

What is it? Where does it live?

What can you tell us about its appearance and behaviour?

Write us a short article. We have hundreds of prizes to give away!

The best entries will also be printed in the magazine.

Age groups: 15–19 and 20 plus.

You have seen this competition in a magazine and decide to enter.

Write your entry for the competition. Your article should be about 150–200 words long.

Don't forget to include:

- why you have chosen the particular creature you are writing about

- what, for you, is special about it

- what can be done to take care of it.

You will receive up to 9 marks for the content of your article, and up to 9 marks for the style and accuracy of your language.

....

....

....

....

....

....

....

....

....

....

....

....

....

....

....

....

....

....

....

....

....

....

....

.... [18]

....

Exercise 7

Your town council is planning to knock down the local museum. Here are some comments from your friends and neighbours about this idea.

'A good idea – it's too old-fashioned and expensive to keep up.'

'It's terrible – that beautiful old building is part of our heritage.'

'People don't need museums any more – a leisure centre would be much more fun!'

'How sad! I love looking at all those wonderful paintings and objects.'

Write a letter to your local newspaper giving your views about the issue. Your letter should be about 150–200 words long.

The comments above may give you some ideas, but you are free to use any ideas of your own.

You will receive up to 9 marks for the content of your letter, and up to 9 marks for the style and accuracy of your language.

....

....

....

....

....

....

....

....

....

....

....

....

....

....

....

....

....

....

....

....

....

....

.... [18]

....

EXTENDED LEVEL

PRACTICE TEST 4

Exercise 1

Read the following advertisement for Dinosaur Farm Museum and then answer the questions on the opposite page.

DINOSAUR FARM MUSEUM
ISLE OF WIGHT

THE WORKING MUSEUM IN THE HEART OF DINOSAUR COUNTRY

The Isle of Wight, off the south coast of England, is the best place in Europe for discovering dinosaur bones. **Dinosaur Farm Museum** was established in 1993, after Europe's most complete Brachiosaurid dinosaur was found here in 1992. Since then, the museum has introduced the study of old bones (paleontology) to many more people.

WHAT WE OFFER

Visitors can enjoy our displays, or watch us cleaning dinosaur bones and other fossils found on the island's beaches. We are proud of our family-friendly atmosphere and knowledgeable staff.

The museum has a variety of different fossils, many of them never displayed to the public before. As more are discovered all the time, you can be sure of seeing something new each time you visit.

We have a free Fossil Identification Service, so you can bring in any fossils you have and find out what they are. In addition, we have a reasonably-priced Museum Shop, where you can buy a souvenir of your visit. You could also bring a picnic and relax in our special picnic area.

ACTIVITIES

Fossil hunts are organised from the museum and run all year round. Groups of up to 25 are guided on a local beach where they can search for fossils. All these hunts are fully licensed and insured, and guides can help to identify any fossils found and point out things of interest.

Due to the popularity of these hunts, all trips must be booked by a personal visit to Dinosaur Farm Museum.

DID YOU KNOW...?

The BBC programme 'Live from Dinosaur Island' was filmed along the coast here, and Dinosaur Farm Museum was the base for the television crew.

FIND OUT MORE

Check out our website at *www.isleofwight.com/dinosaurfarm* to learn in detail how we dig for dinosaurs. You can also read about the many different kinds of dinosaurs which lived in this area, which was connected to Europe 120 million years ago. Or, better still, visit us at *Military Road, near Brighstone, Isle of Wight PO30 4PG.*

a) When did the museum open?

.... [1]

b) What is remarkable about the Brachiosaurid dinosaur found on the Isle of Wight?

.... [1]

c) What activity can visitors observe to give them a better understanding of old bones?

.... [1]

d) Why are parents with young children likely to find their visit enjoyable and relaxing?

.... [1]

e) Why are there always new things to see at the museum?

.... [1]

f) Where do the fossil hunts take place?

.... [1]

g) How can you book a fossil hunt?

.... [1]

h) Name **two** things that visitors to the website can read about.

.... [1]

[Total: 8]

Exercise 2

Read the following newspaper article about the numbers of people learning English around the world. Then answer the questions on the opposite page.

THE GLOBAL LANGUAGE

According to research, published in a recent report *The Future of English*, half the world's population will be speaking or learning English by 2015. It is thought that two billion people will start learning English within ten years or so, and three billion will be able to speak it.

The research was based on a computer model which was developed to estimate the demand for English language teaching around the world. The model charts likely student numbers up to 2050.

The report's author, David Graddol, looked at various estimates from different countries. Amongst other factors, he found that many governments are now introducing the teaching of English, even at kindergarten level, because of its economic importance. English predominates in the world of business, with many countries wishing to compete for financially important manufacturing contracts. However, countries such as Malaysia and Sri Lanka are, at the same time, protecting their native languages, which are closely identified with their national independence and identity.

According to the report, the current rapid growth in English learning around the world is the result of increased numbers of primary school children and middle-aged people being taught the subject for the first time. Other languages such as French may be at risk from this trend, but the report predicts that the boom will be over by 2050, when English-language students will be down from two billion to 500 million. The English-language teaching business will become the victim of its own success, and will therefore gradually decline over time.

As more of the world's youngest children learn English as their second language, fewer of them will need to be taught it later in their school careers, as they will already have reached high levels of proficiency. They will even be expected to start learning other school subjects such as maths and science through the medium of English.

Many universities are also choosing to teach through English, with students expected to listen to, read and write very high-level subjects in English instead of their own languages. Many people in the world will thus have achieved a high level of competence in English, and numbers of learners will begin to fall.

Mr Graddol points out that Britain has not got a very good reputation for learning other languages, so may be at a disadvantage in the future. Valuable business may move away from Britain to countries where more people are bilingual or multi-lingual, skills which are highly prized. The report also shows that English is not the only language spreading across the world. Far from being dominated by English, the world will become more multi-lingual. Chinese, Arabic and Spanish are all popular, and likely to be languages of the future. This is something students worldwide will need to think about when planning their careers.

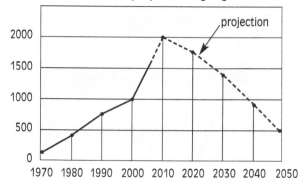

Millions of people learning English

Adapted from an article by James Burleigh, © The Independent 2004.

(a) According to the article, how many people will be learning English by 2015?

.... [1]

(b) What was the purpose of David Graddol's research?

.... [1]

(c) Why is the number of English learners increasing? Give **two** reasons.

....

.... [2]

(d) Why are some countries protecting their native languages against the impact of English?

.... [1]

(e) Name **two** ways in which education will be different for young people who learned English at primary school?

....

.... [2]

(f) According to the graph, in which year will the number of English learners reach a peak?

.... [1]

(g) What will happen by 2050?

.... [1]

(h) Why will there be a demand for bilingual and multi-lingual speakers?

.... [1]

(i) Make a list of **four** difficulties Britain could have in the future, according to the article.

- ....

- ....

- ....

- .... [4]

[Total: 14]

Exercise 3

Amir Begadi is a very keen seventeen-year-old musician in the orchestra at the Northern College in Bulgaria. The college is situated at Burgas Avenue, Sofia. The orchestra is called the Northern College Amateur Orchestra and has 24 members, plus their conductor Mr Ivanov. Their email address is orchestra@n.college.ac.bg.

Amir is the Principal Violinist, and also organises the rehearsals and concerts. He is in the process of organising a visit to Romania, where the orchestra will take part in an international student orchestra contest. There will be young musicians and college orchestras from all over the world.

The competition will take place in Bucharest over three days, Monday 3rd – Wednesday 5th August, but Amir's group will arrive on the Sunday to prepare for the competition and to settle in. They will be travelling to Romania in two minibuses with their instruments, and they will take sleeping bags with them, as they are planning to camp indoors in the Sports Halls provided by the Romanian organisers.

The members of the orchestra had hoped to take part in one of the guided cultural excursions plus picnic lunch being offered by the city of Bucharest on Thursday 6th July – they are particularly interested in visiting the National Art Museum and the Cotroceni Palace Museum. However, as the group has to travel home on the Wednesday evening, after the final concert, they plan to make their own sightseeing arrangements. They hope they will have time to visit one or both museums sometime on the second day of their stay, between rehearsals.

The orchestra are keen to get at least second or third place in the competition, which would be an improvement on their last competition, in France. They also hope to play one of the pieces which has been specially composed for them by Mrs Daimler, Head of Music at the college. It will be the first time the piece has been played in public, and the orchestra are excited about having this opportunity.

Mrs Daimler and Mr Ivanov will be accompanying them to Bucharest and are helping Amir with the arrangements.

Imagine you are Amir, and complete the competition entry form on the opposite page, using the information above.

25TH INTERNATIONAL STUDENT ORCHESTRA COMPETITION
ENTRY FORM

School/college name and address (*Please use BLOCK CAPITALS*):

_____

_____

Name of orchestra: _____

Contact person/organiser: _____

Email: _____

Age: _____   Male / Female (*Delete as necessary*)

Position in orchestra: _____

Number of players in orchestra: _____

Name(s) of accompanying teacher(s)/staff member(s):

_____

Arrival date: _____

Type of accommodation required. *Please circle*:

    Hotel   Youth hostel   Indoor camping   Campsite

Number of nights accommodation required: _____

Is this the first time your orchestra has taken part in
a competition outside your own country?   Yes / No (*Delete as necessary*)

Do members of your group wish to be included in any
of the guided excursions on Thursday 6th August,
followed by a picnic lunch?   Yes / No (*Delete as necessary*)

If Yes, please tick to show which trips you are interested in:
❏ Guided tour of Cotroceni Palace Museum   ❏ Trip to National Art Museum
❏ Excursion to Snagov Lake and Monastery

Please write one sentence of **12–20 words** describing what the orchestra members hope to gain from the experience.

_____

_____

[Total: 8]

Exercise 4

Read the following article about vultures, large birds which feed on dead animals. Then complete the notes on the opposite page.

WHY INDIA NEEDS ITS DYING VULTURES

They may look ugly and threatening, but the sudden steep decline in three species of India's vultures is producing alarm rather than celebration, and it presents the world with a new kind of environmental problem. The dramatic decline in vulture numbers is causing widespread disruption to people living in the same areas as the birds, as well as serious public health problems across the Indian sub-continent.

While their reputation and appearance may be unpleasant, scruffy and scary to Western eyes, vultures have long played a very important role in keeping towns and villages all over India clean, by feeding on dead cows. In India, cows are sacred animals and are traditionally left in the open when they die in their thousands every year.

The disappearance of the vultures has led to an explosion in the numbers of wild dogs feasting on the remains of these dead animals. There are fears that rabies may increase as a result, and ultimately affect humans in the region, since wild dogs are the main carriers of this terrifying disease. Rabies could also spread to other animal species, causing an even greater problem in the future.

The need for action is urgent, so an emergency project has been launched to find a solution by trying to identify the disease causing the birds' deaths and, if possible, develop a cure. The project will be run in a Vulture Care Centre in Haryana, north of Delhi, and will be financed by the Darwin Initiative, an international wildlife grants programme.

The three species of vulture affected are the long-billed, the slender-billed and the Indian white-backed vulture. Experts think a virus may be responsible, although no one has found proof of this yet. It is feared that the disease could also spread to other parts of the world, including Africa and Europe.

Large-scale vulture deaths were first noticed at the end of the 1980s in India's Keoladeo National Park. The birds were lacking in energy, with drooping necks, dying after several weeks of sickness. Then reports began to come in of vulture deaths all across India. A population survey at that time showed that the white-backed species had declined by 96 per cent, while the other species had declined by 92 per cent. All three species are now listed as 'critically endangered'.

As most vultures lay only single eggs and take about five years to reach maturity, reversing this population decline will be a long and difficult exercise.

Adapted from an article by Michael McCarthy, © The Independent 2003.

You are preparing to give a talk to your class about India's endangered vultures. Make short notes under the headings below.

WHY THE DISEASE IS A SERIOUS PROBLEM

- .... [1]

- .... [1]

- .... [1]

PROPOSED WORK OF THE VULTURE CARE CENTRE

- .... [1]

SYMPTOMS OF THE DISEASE

- .... [1]

- .... [1]

RATE OF VULTURE DECLINE

- .... [1]

- .... [1]

[Total: 8]

Exercise 5

Read the following talk about colour therapy, and then write a summary about how colour affects our lives.

Your summary should be about 100 words. You should use your own words as far as possible.

You will receive up to 6 marks for the content of your summary, and up to 4 marks for the style and accuracy of your language.

COLOUR THERAPY

You might think that whether you choose a blue shirt or a yellow one to wear to work or college makes no difference to your day and those around you. However, an increasing number of experts argue that the colours we choose affect our mood, our career prospects and even our health.

The power of colour has been used for centuries and we should be making the most of it in our lives today. Colour affects us to a greater degree than most of us realise. It is used increasingly by psychologists and therapists for influencing mood and state of mind, and for various types of treatments when we are ill. Some people even believe that the blind can benefit from the 'vibrations' that colour gives off.

Companies use colour to great effect to encourage us to buy their products. For example, purple is seen as creative and mixes well with red, to show that a company has ideas and the power to make them happen. Orange and blue are also recommended colours for companies to use, because orange is the colour of communication and blue suggests safety and security. So this could be a particularly good combination. Companies have found that certain colours 'speak' to specific age groups. They often use red to attract younger people

to their products, for example, as it is vibrant and more youthful than colours like gold and navy, which older customers seem to prefer.

Wearing different colours can affect how you feel and how others react to you, so it is important to consider this when deciding what to wear in the morning. If you want people to take you seriously, then wearing navy blue or black is good. Blue would also be helpful for an interview or oral examination because it relaxes you and makes you feel calm. Red gets you noticed by everyone and makes you, the wearer, feel energetic, but be careful, as it can raise your pulse rate and not everyone wants this effect.

Turquoise is a 'user-friendly', approachable colour, which people are attracted to; they feel friendly towards you when you wear it. It is also thought that turquoise can treat stress and headaches. Green is a good colour if you are not feeling well, and possibly this is why we sometimes give flowers and plants to friends and relatives in hospital.

So think carefully before you leave the house or visit a friend with a gift. The colours you choose in both cases are a powerful tool. Are you making the right impression – on yourself and on others?

....

....

....

....

....

....

....

....

....

....

....

....

....

....

....

....

....

....

....

....

....

.... [10]

Exercise 6

> # REGIONAL BUILDING FUND – GRANTS AVAILABLE
>
> **DOES YOUR TOWN NEED A NEW SWIMMING POOL, A CLINIC, A COLLEGE, A LIBRARY, A SITE FOR LOCAL INDUSTRY...?**
>
> Did you know that money could be granted to your town from the Regional Building Fund? Write to your Town Hall with your views and suggestions.

You have seen the above advertisement in your local paper and decide to write a letter suggesting a new building for your town.

Your letter should be about 150–200 words long.

Don't forget to include:

- your suggested building

- why your town needs it

- where this building should be located.

You will receive up to 9 marks for the content of your letter, and up to 9 marks for the style and accuracy of your language.

....

....

....

....

....

....

....

....

....

....

....

....

....

....

....

....

....

....

....

....

.... [18]

Exercise 7

Your college is planning to cut music, orchestra and choir lessons from the timetable from the beginning of next year. Here are some comments about this from students and their parents:

'We won't be able to play the violin together as part of an orchestra anymore.'

'I wanted to become a professional musician — now I won't have a chance!'

'I'm glad. Music takes up too much of the school timetable – we need more time for extra English lessons.'

'If you want to play an instrument, you can do it at home.'

'What a pity! My daughter really enjoys singing in the choir. There's too much emphasis on academic subjects.'

Write an article for your college magazine giving your views about this issue.
Your article should be about 150–200 words long.

The comments above may give you some ideas, but you are free to use any ideas of your own.

You will receive up to 9 marks for the content of your article, and up to 9 marks for the style and accuracy of your language.

....

....

....

....

....

....

....

....

....

....

....

....

....

....

....

....

....

....

....

....

....

....

.... [18]

KEY

Marking the language aspect of the summary

Use the table below as a guide to help you focus on specific elements when marking the fluency, cohesion and clarity of the students' answers. Award marks according to the table.

4 marks	1 mark
The student has excellent language skills and resources and is able to write a coherent, sustained summary, mainly in his/her own words. He/she shows analytical skills in interpreting the task. The writing flows well, with smooth linking between ideas. These are expressed concisely and there is a strong sense of summary style. The summary is close to the word limit and may be divided into more than one paragraph if appropriate (Extended canditates only). Ambitious vocabulary, however, or elaborate sentence constructions are not necessary for full marks.	The student's writing shows some understanding of the text and the question set, but overall the writing is too general and shows little sense of an appropriate summary style. The standard of language is weak. There may be mistakes in basic construction, punctuation or spelling so that occasionally the meaning is unclear. There are few or no connectors and/or they may be used incorrectly. This gives the writing a rambling effect. There may be a tendency to write a simple list of items or to copy a substantial amount from the text. Some of the material in the summary may be unconnected to the question. This may include ideas not given in the text, and the student's own opinions. There is no attempt to keep to the word limit.
3 marks	**0 marks**
The student shows a good understanding of the text and the task set, and writes with a high degree of organisation and control. Sentences are usually straightforward and accurate, and the meaning is clear. There is little misspelling. Some connectors are used to link ideas and to help make the summary coherent and orderly. The student has sufficient language resources and breadth of vocabulary to put ideas from the text into his/her own words quite often.	The content of what the student has written is completely irrelevant and shows no understanding of the text or the question set. His/her language errors are so numerous as to make communication incomprehensible.
2 marks	
The student makes some attempt to respond accurately to the task and to develop a clear, organised summary using some connectors. There may, however, be lapses where pieces are copied from the original text, and some of the copying may contain irrelevance. Basic punctuation, such as capitals and full stops, is accurate, and simple words are spelled accurately. Sentence construction is generally satisfactory, but limited language resources and response to the task may produce, overall, a fragmented effect.	

Marking exercises 6 and 7

Note: At Core level, up to 5 marks are available for content and up to 5 marks for language. At Extended level, up to 9 marks are available for each.

Marks	CONTENT: Relevance and development of ideas	Marks	LANGUAGE: Style and accuracy
8–9	**Highly effective** *Relevance:* Fulfils the task, with consistently appropriate register, and excellent sense of purpose and audience. *Development of ideas:* Shows independence of thought. Ideas are well developed, at appropriate length and persuasive. Quality is sustained throughout. Enjoyable to read. The interest of the reader is aroused and sustained.	8–9	**Fluent** *Style:* Almost first language competence. Ease of style. Confident and wide-ranging use of language, idiom and tenses. *Accuracy:* No or very few errors. Well-constructed and linked paragraphs.
6–7	**Effective** *Relevance:* Fulfils the task, with appropriate register and good sense of purpose and audience. *Development of ideas:* Ideas are well developed and at appropriate length. Engages reader's interest.	6–7	**Precise** *Style:* Sentences show variety of structure and length. Some style and turn of phrase. Uses some idioms and is precise in use of vocabulary. However, there may be some awkwardness in style, making reading less enjoyable. *Accuracy:* Generally accurate, apart from occasional frustrating minor errors. There are paragraphs showing some unity, although links may be absent or inappropriate.
4–5	**Satisfactory** *Relevance:* Fulfils the task, with reasonable attempt at appropriate register, and some sense of purpose and audience. A satisfactory attempt has been made to address the topic, but there may be digressions. *Development of ideas:* Material is satisfactorily developed at appropriate length.	4–5	**Safe** *Style:* Mainly simple structures and vocabulary, sometimes attempting more sophisticated language. *Accuracy:* Meaning is clear, and work is of a safe, literate standard. Simple structures are generally sound, apart from infrequent spelling errors, which do not interfere with communication. Grammatical errors occur when more sophistication is attempted. Paragraphs are used but without coherence or unity.
2–3	**Partly relevant** *Relevance:* Partly relevant and some engagement with the task. Does not quite fulfil the task, although there are some positive qualities. Inappropriate register, showing insufficient awareness of purpose and/or audience. *Development of ideas:* Supplies some detail and explanation, but the effect is incomplete. Some repetition.	2–3	**Errors intrude** *Style:* Simple structures and vocabulary. *Accuracy:* Meaning is sometimes in doubt. Frequent, distracting errors hamper precision and slow down reading. However, these do not seriously impair communication. Paragraphs absent or haphazard.
0–1	**Little relevance** Limited engagement with the task, but this is mostly hidden by density of error. **(Award 1 mark.)** No engagement with the task, or any engagement with the task is completely hidden by density of error. **(Award 0 marks.)** If essay is completely irrelevant, no mark can be given for language.	0–1	**Hard to understand** Multiple types of error in grammar/spelling/word usage/punctuation throughout which mostly make understanding difficult. Sense can be deciphered occasionally. Paragraphs absent or inconsistent. **(Award 1 mark.)** Density of error completely obscures meaning. Whole sections impossible to recognise as pieces of English writing. Paragraphs absent or inconsistent. **(Award 0 marks.)**

PRACTICE TEST 1 (CORE LEVEL)

Exercise 1 *[6 marks]*

(a) (Europe's deepest) seawater aquarium
(b) only one in the world
(c) submarine and viewing tunnel *(both needed)*
(d) marine dinosaur wall
(e) 5 pm
(f) the marina

Exercise 2 *[10 marks]*

(a) roofing and fencing *(both needed)*
(b) It became a vital ingredient in many things.
(c) *Any 2 of:* Plant became weaker / Plant became diseased / Attempts to save it were useless / Problems of the plant could get worse (in the future).
(d) They mixed genes from wild and commercial types.
(e) It makes the plant resistant to rust.
(f) Brazil, Mexico, Australia
(g) *Any 4 of:*
  • New/Barbados type contains 5% more sugar.
  • The plant is now stronger/healthier/ more vigorous/more disease-resistant
  • International research is working on improving the plant.
  • Gene for rust resistance has been identified.
  • Supply is more guaranteed.

Exercise 3 *[10 marks]*

See completed form on page 89.

Exercise 4 *[6 marks]*
Similarities between people and dolphins

Any 2 of:
• great communicators
• work together
• have own language dialect
• pass down knowledge from one generation to next

Practical ways dolphins have helped people

Any 2 of:
• helped fishermen
• protected them from sharks
• saved them from drowning

How people threaten their survival

Any 2 of:
• drowning in fishing nets
• pollution
• noise

Exercise 5 *[4 marks]*

Up to 4 marks are given for language. Use the table on page 82 as a guide.
Model summary

Dolphins and people are alike in the way they love to communicate, and the way they live in families and cooperate to achieve shared goals. Dolphins have shown a protective instinct to humans by rescuing them from drowning and from sharks. They have also helped fishermen to catch fish. Sadly, people threaten dolphins through sea pollution, accidentally trapping them in fishing nets and by bombarding them with noise. *(68 words)*

Exercise 6 *[10 marks]*
Content and language

Up to 5 marks for each. Use the table on page 83 as a guide.
A model composition is provided on page 94.

Exercise 7 *[10 marks]*
Content and language

Up to 5 marks for each. Use the table on page 83 as a guide.
A model composition is provided on page 94.

PRACTICE TEST 2

Exercise 1 *[8 marks]*

(a) *Any 2 of:* light / sound / special effects
(b) from the (tour) guides
(c) space experiments
(d) get inside model of Space Shuttle
(e) to reinforce what has been learned
(f) covered area
(g) Mondays except in school holidays
(h) telephone +32-61-65-133

Exercise 2 *[14 marks]*

(a) They are now guaranteed a fair price for their honey.
(b) It is 60 miles from a telephone or electricity source.
(c) from the forest and rivers
(d) his small house and two bicycles
(e) He can send them to school, and pay for medical care.
(f) with a cylinder of bark, hung in a tree
(g) The bees feed on wild flowers (including orchids).
(h) The honey can be eaten 'within a month'.
(i) *All 6 of:*
   • Gather leafy branches and make them into a bundle.
   • Add dry reeds and light them.
   • Climb up the tree to the hive.
   • Wave smoke into the hive to make the bees calm.
   • Take out the honeycomb.
   • Sell directly to the buyer from North West Bee Products.

Exercise 3 *[8 marks]*

See completed form on page 90.

Exercise 4 *[8 marks]*

Examples of the use of watercress through the ages:

• Romans ate watercress as a cure for baldness.

• Watercress sandwiches/'poor man's bread' eaten for breakfast in 19th-century Europe.
• Celebrities use watercress-soup diet to lose weight.

Health-giving properties of watercress:

• Contains vitamins C, K and A.
• Contains iron, potassium, copper and calcium.

Buying and eating watercress:

• the best: silky green unmarked leaves, crisp undamaged stems
• older watercress: darker leaves and thicker stems
• young watercress: grown for 28 days / mild flavour

Exercise 5 *[10 marks]*

Content

One mark for each correct point, up to 6 marks.

Born to trade

• trade goes back to dawn/birth of humanity
• existed before writing/laws/cities/farming metal tools
• natural to exchange food and simple tools for survival, e.g. axes/fish hooks
• natural human ability to keep record of credits and debits
• economic benefits hard to resist / everyone involved made a profit
• 'consumer culture'/trade in luxury items older than first thought
• art/jewellery/cosmetics/decorative objects found in Africa go back 76,000–100,000 years
• early trade prepared way for modern shopping equivalent

Language

Up to 4 marks. Use the table on page 82 as a guide.

Model summary

The idea of buying or trading items began with the

birth of mankind. People traded or exchanged food and simple tools to ensure survival before cities were built, farming began or laws were established. Money was not used – items such as fish hooks and axe heads were simply exchanged.

The desire to trade and the ability to keep records of transactions were as natural in ancient times as now. Even luxury items such as jewellery were traded at least 76,000 years ago, as archaeological evidence shows. This early trading eventually gave rise to our modern way of shopping. *(98 words)*

Exercise 6 *[18 marks]*
Content and language

Up to 9 marks for each. Use the table on page 83 as a guide.
A model composition is provided on page 94.

Exercise 7 *[18 marks]*
Content and language

Up to 9 marks for each. Use the table on page 83 as a guide.
A model composition is provided on page 95.

PRACTICE TEST 3

Exercise 1 *[8 marks]*

(a) *Any 2 of:* world's smallest frog / world's heaviest land tortoise / only flightless bird of the Indian Ocean
(b) many different races (have come to the islands)
(c) (228 sq km) Marine National Park
(d) take home rubbish/toothpaste cartons/ shampoo bottles *(at least 1 example of rubbish must be included)*
(e) trade winds
(f) March to May and September to November
(g) June and July
(h) valid yellow fever vaccination certificate

Exercise 2 *[14 marks]*

(a) African Elephant Conservation Trust
(b) *Any 3 of:* gentle / sensitive / caring / fearless / leader
(c) She got 3 other elephants to help track and rescue her kidnapped baby / She took on a mother's role when older members of her family died.
(d) famine and drought *(both needed)*
(e) *Any 2 of:* poaching / hunting / destroying habitat
(f) They support it.

(g) family structure is being preserved / wide age range
(h) more about the Trust's work, more about Echo and her family *(both points)*
(i) *All 6 of:*
  • birth rates
  • death rates
  • sophisticated communication
  • they celebrate birth
  • lifelong friendships
  • they mourn death of family members

Exercise 3 *[8 marks]*

See completed form on page 91.

Exercise 4 *[8 marks]*
Effects of dehydration during exercise

• You overheat.
• Heart pumps faster.
• Exercise becomes more difficult/requires more effort.

Why we may not get enough fluids during exercise

• Thirst mechanism doesn't work properly / We don't notice we are thirsty.

- The body doesn't absorb water properly / Stomach becomes intolerant to fluids.

How to avoid dehydration during exercise

Any 3 of:
- Manage your intake properly.
  Drink regular small amounts.
- Drink before you start exercising.
- Match your intake to the kind of exercise you are doing / Drink about two litres for one hour of exercise.

Exercise 5 *[10 marks]*

Content

One mark for each correct point, up to 6 marks.

Why perfume manufacturers use artificial ingredients

- Scientific developments have made substitutes for natural ingredients possible.
- complementary to natural ingredients
- acceptable to the consumer
- supply of natural ingredients insufficient to meet demand
- reduces costs / natural ingredients very expensive
- gives manufacturers more control over the production process / no longer affected by weather/pests/crop yields, etc

Language

Up to 4 marks. Use the table on page 82 as a guide.

Model summary

Advances in science and technology mean that perfume manufacturers can make artificial scents and mix them with natural oils to produce a perfume that the public will like and enjoy using. A further reason for the growing popularity of artificial ingredients is that it cuts down to some extent on the expense of the manufacturing process. Finally, artificial elements enable manufacturers to plan production without excessive worry that natural ingredients may not be available or that their supply may be reduced because of bad weather, a poor harvest or attack by pests. *(92 words)*

Exercise 6 *[18 marks]*
Content and language

Up to 9 marks for each. Use the table on page 83 as a guide.
A model composition is provided on page 95.

Exercise 7 *[18 marks]*
Content and language

Up to 9 marks for each. Use the table on page 83 as a guide.
A model composition is provided on page 95.

PRACTICE TEST 4

Exercise 1 *[8 marks]*
(a) 1993
(b) most complete in Europe
(c) cleaning bones (and other fossils)
(d) family-friendly atmosphere
(e) more fossils are discovered all the time
(f) on a local beach
(g) by a personal visit to the museum
(h) how the museum digs for dinosaurs; kinds of dinosaurs that lived in the area *(both needed)*

Exercise 2 *[14 marks]*
(a) 2 billion
(b) To estimate the demand for English language teaching around the world.
(c) *Any 2 of:* More primary school children are learning English / More middle-aged people are learning English / Governments are introducing the teaching of English.
(d) Because the languages are closely identified with the countries' national independence/ identity.

(e) *Both of:*
They won't need to learn it later in their academic careers.
They will learn other subjects through (the medium of) English.

(f) 2010

(g) The number of English learners will fall/decrease to 500 million.

(h) These skills are highly prized in business.

(i) *All 4 of:*
- The English-language teaching boom will be over.
- Valuable business could move away from Britain.
- The world will become more multi-lingual (and British people are not good at learning other languages).
- Other languages could spread across the world (such as Chinese, Arabic and Spanish).

Exercise 3 *[8 marks]*

See completed form on page 92.

Exercise 4 *[8 marks]*

Why the disease is a serious problem

- More wild dogs, causing increase in rabies in humans.
- Other animals could catch rabies.
- Vulture disease might spread to other countries (Africa/Europe).

Proposed work of the Vulture Care Centre

- identify the disease / develop a cure

Symptoms of the disease

- lack of energy
- drooping neck

Rate of vulture decline

- white-backed – 96 per cent
- other (2) species – 92 per cent

Editor's note: Since the article was written, scientists have reported that the cause of the vultures' deaths is a drug used for the treatment of sick cattle – it kills vultures that feed on the bodies of animals treated with the drug. It is now hoped that Indian farmers will use an alternative drug that is not toxic to vultures.

Exercise 5 *[10 marks]*

Content

One mark for each correct point, up to 6 marks.

How colour affects our lives

- affects mood/state of mind/how you feel
- affects career prospects
- affects health / helps when we are ill
- companies use colour to get people to buy their products
- affects how others see us/react to us
- need to consider what colours we wear
- need to consider colour when giving gifts

Language

Up to 4 marks. Use the table on page 82 as a guide.

Model summary

It is thought that colour affects our health, our career and how we feel. Some people believe that it can even help cure illnesses. Companies use colour to make us buy things and to appeal to different kinds of customers. Wearing certain colours can affect our performance in interviews or examinations, and it can affect how others behave towards us. Giving gifts should be carefull considered, as the colour reflects our attitude and can have an effect on whoever receives the gift. Even people who cannot see may be affected by the vibrations that colours emit. *(96 words)*

Exercise 6 *[18 marks]*

Content and language

Up to 9 marks for each. Use the table on page 8: as a guide.
A model composition is provided on page 96.

Exercise 7 *[18 marks]*

Content and language

Up to 9 marks for each. Use the table on page 8: as a guide.
A model composition is provided on page 96.

GLOBAL ECO-PROJECTS

VOLUNTEER APPLICATION FORM / MALDIVES

(Please give your full name and address in CAPITAL LETTERS.)

NAME _LINDY MELAMU_

ADDRESS _984 TEMBENKO ROAD, GABORONE,_

BOTSWANA

TELEPHONE _267-3901278_   EMAIL _melamu.l@remac.com_

Please circle your age group: (16–19)   19–21   21–24   Over 24

~~Male~~ / Female   (please delete)

How did you find out about Global Eco-Projects?

Advert on the Internet

Are you intending to travel alone?   Yes / ~~No~~   (please delete)

If you have a preference for any particular project, please specify:

Restoring coral reefs

Please specify any special dietary requirements: _I am a vegetarian._

Do you have any medical conditions the organisers should be aware of? _No_

Which time(s) of the year are you available? _Beginning December to end March_

In the space below, please write **one sentence** giving information about any experience you have of environmental work, and **one sentence** explaining what you hope to gain from the project.

I have helped to turn waste ground into a farm growing fruit and vegetables

for local people. I would like the opportunity to travel to such a beautiful part

of the world, and to learn more about nature and environmental work.

Test 1, Exercise 3

[Total: 10]

ANTWERP ARTIST OF THE YEAR

*Please complete all of **Part A** in CAPITALS.*

PART A

Name of artist ...JEANNE LAVALE...

Age ...18........................

Number of years of formal art study ...2...

School/College attended ...ART DECO COLLEGE OF ART & DESIGN................

Address ...27 TERVURENLAAN, ANTWERP...

PART B

Media/materials used for competition artworks. *Please circle as many as required:*

Oils   Acrylics   (Watercolours)   Charcoal   Clay   Stone   (Metal)   (Wood)   Plastic   Other (*Please specify*) ....

I wish to enter the following
artworks for the competition: Name of Painting 1 ...Julie................................

Name of Painting 2 ...Home................................

Name of Sculpture ...Machine Mind........................

PART C

Complete as appropriate: I wish to   (a) have my artworks collected on ...17th...... July.

or   (b) deliver them to the Kattenberg Studio on .... July.

If you have chosen (a), please provide: College contact number ...571-9300, ext.403.........

Name of member of staff ...Mrs V. Bernet.......................

PART D

In no more than 20 words, use the box below to tell us how you would use the prize money.

It would help me to continue working as an artist, and also to start
a painting workshop for young children.

LOCAL TOWNS FACT-FINDING SURVEY

Please help us to find out more about the opinions of residents in local towns by completing this survey form.

SECTION 1

Please write your name and address in block capitals.

Name: _CHEN LEE_

Address : _21 ORANGE TREE AVENUE, OAKTON_

Age: _16_   Occupation: _Student_

Approximately how long have you lived in the town? _6 years_

If you have lived in the town for less than three years, please write your previous address:

Approximate population of your town. (*Please circle.*)

Under 12000   12000–15000   15000–25000   (25000–40000)   More than 40000

Approximate number of homes. (*Please delete numbers not applicable.*)

~~Fewer than 3000~~   ~~3000–6000~~   6000–12000   ~~12000–24000~~   ~~More than 24000~~

How did you come to live in the town? (*Please tick.*)

☐ Born here   ☑ Came with family   ☐ Other
☐ Got employment in area   ☐ Marriage
☐ Retired here   ☐ Attracted by peacefulness of area

Which of the following facilities in your town do you use on a regular basis? (Please tick.)

☐ Sports Centre   ☑ Swimming Pool   ☑ Cafés/Restaurants
☐ Cinema   ☑ Recreation Ground/Park   ☑ Clubs

Do you do any voluntary work in the town? (Yes) / No   (*Please circle.*)

If Yes, give details: _I help with our Good Neighbour Scheme._

From the following list, tick **three** items that are most important to you for future development in your town.

☐ More extensive recycling facilities   ☑ More nature conservation areas   ☑ Better choice of shops
☐ Improved transport connections   ☐ Wider use of road safety cameras
☑ Facilities for teenagers   ☐ Restriction on the building of new houses

SECTION 2

The government wishes to increase industrial development and needs to identify suitable places for this in the local region. Write one sentence of **12–20 words** saying how you would feel about more industrial development in your town.

I would be happy to see another factory built in Oakton, as it would provide jobs for young people.

Test 3, Exercise 3   [Total: 8]

25TH INTERNATIONAL STUDENT ORCHESTRA COMPETITION
ENTRY FORM

School/college name and address (*Please use BLOCK CAPITALS*):

NORTHERN COLLEGE, BURGAS AVENUE,

SOFIA, BULGARIA

Name of orchestra: Northern College Amateur Orchestra

Contact person/organiser: Amir Begadi

Email: orchestra@n.college.ac.bg

Age: 17   Male / ~~Female~~ (*Delete as necessary*)

Position in orchestra: Principal Violinist

Number of players in orchestra: 24

Name(s) of accompanying teacher(s)/staff member(s):

Mr Ivanov & Mrs Daimler

Arrival date: 2nd August

Type of accommodation required. *Please circle*:

Hotel   Youth hostel   (Indoor camping)   Campsite

Number of nights accommodation required: 3

Is this the first time your orchestra has taken part in
a competition outside your own country?   ~~Yes~~ / No (*Delete as necessary*)

Do members of your group wish to be included in any
of the guided excursions on Thursday 6th August,
followed by a picnic lunch?   ~~Yes~~ / No (*Delete as necessary*)

If Yes, please tick to show which trips you are interested in:
❏ Guided tour of Cotroceni Palace Museum   ❏ Trip to National Art Museum
❏ Excursion to Snagov Lake and Monastery

Please write one sentence of **12–20 words** describing what the orchestra members hope to gain from the experience.

We hope to play a piece composed by our teacher, and also improve our performance in our last competition / get at least third place in the competition.

Test 4, Exercise 3   [Total: 8]

MODEL COMPOSITIONS

PRACTICE TEST 1 (CORE LEVEL)

Exercise 6 *(page 28)*

I am an enthusiastic, fun-loving student at Greenpark College. My main subject is English, and I have been writing short stories for the class Writing Group for about four years. I would love to be considered as one of your regular writers.

My first love is writing, but I also enjoy talking to other people and contacting them on the Internet to find out what they think. I am always interested in what the rest of the college are concerned about, from student worries to world events.

Mostly I like to write about things that are happening in the college, like sports events, trips to places of interest, and hints on getting better grades. I am pretty fluent in English, and my teachers say my style and presentation are good.

It would give me such a boost to see my words in print. I'd love to be involved. *(148 words)*

Exercise 7 *(page 30)*

Many of us have never been abroad, so I think the idea of sending a school sports team overseas is brilliant. We can learn so much from travel and meeting other people – even being on a plane will be new and thrilling.

Furthermore, I think travel can make us more tolerant and understanding of people who have different cultures and customs. We'll have the opportunity to make new friendships that could last the rest of our lives.

Some people are worried that it will be hard to compete abroad because the food and climate could be really different. In my opinion, this is a challenge, not a serious problem. We're all adaptable, and I think the new environment could improve our sports performance.

To sum up, I think everyone should relax and concentrate on the wonderful opportunity this will be for those who are lucky enough to be selected. *(149 words)*

PRACTICE TEST 2

Exercise 6 *(page 44)*

(Dear Editor,)

I was shocked to read in your paper that our local railway line is to be closed at the end of the year. The line has served us for many years, and generations of people have used it for journeys to and from work and college. As you know, it connects to the main line and takes commuters, travellers and tourists to the capital. It is also the boat train – the only connection with the ferry to our island.

If the line closes, countless students from our town will have to cycle or walk through lanes to college, whereas at the moment the train takes them there every 30 minutes. The twice-daily bus service which covers this route is not satisfactory, the journey takes much longer, and the fare is double that of the train. In addition, many students already hold valid season tickets for the train for a period beyond the proposed shut-down. Finally, the line provides work for many local people, and also brings tourists to our town, helping our shops and businesses economically.

As a solution, I suggest that the line stays open but that fewer trains are run at off-peak times, thereby covering costs.

(Yours faithfully,) *(198 words)*

Exercise 7 *(page 46)*

I think having at least one good teacher is very important. He or she can give you motivation to do well, even in a subject you may not always find easy.

If you get on with your teachers, then learning becomes fun. You won't even notice all the hard work you are doing, and your grades will improve. On the other hand, if you find it hard to like your teachers, life at school or college will be awful and you will struggle to do even the simplest things. You'll feel you can't succeed at anything, no matter how hard you try.

The teacher who helped me most was my English teacher, Mrs Kelly. She was always very kind and made the lessons clear and amusing. I remember we laughed a lot in her classes and looked forward to them. Now I want to be a teacher just like her, and I hope I will have her sense of humour and give the same help to students that she gave to us.

Thank goodness I have good teachers and supportive parents, so that I will be able to achieve my aims – if I work hard too! *(196 words)*

PRACTICE TEST 3

Exercise 6 *(page 60)*

Most people love their family pets but I think my spaniel Joey is one hundred per cent perfect. Not only is he faithful and friendly, but he hardly ever barks, even when he is hungry or worried. The really unusual thing about him is that, although he was ill-treated as a puppy and has a horrible scar near his eye as a result, he never shows aggression or bad temper.

We got Joey from an animal sanctuary and, as soon as I saw his big, sad, brown eyes looking at me from behind the bars of his cage, I knew he was for us.

Taking care of him is easy. Apart from eating and drinking almost anything, his favourite activity is going out for walks. When he sees me getting the dog lead, he rushes outside wagging his tail and jumping for joy. Despite being six years old, Joey is still full of energy and mischief. He enjoys chasing rabbits and even tries to follow them down rabbit holes!

All in all, Joey is a special dog because he has overcome a bad start in life and developed a gentle and exuberant nature. We adore him! *(196 words)*

Exercise 7 *(page 62)*

(Dear Editor,)

I was very surprised to read that the council is planning to knock down the Arts and Crafts Museum in the Town Square.

In my opinion this would be quite wrong, as we would lose a beautiful old building that is an important part of the history of our town. Many of the paintings in the museum show what the town was like in earlier periods. I find it fascinating to see the clothes and tools my great-great-grandparents might have had. I also really like the special shoe collection which comes from the time when the wealth of the town was based on shoe manufacture.

Some local residents say museums are boring, but they needn't be. Instead of destroying the museum completely, why not modernise it? We could have interactive displays, computers, a café and regular talks from experts. If it felt more up-to-date and user-friendly, no-one would question its value.

Finally, although it's true that the town needs a swimming pool, it should be built in addition to the museum, not instead of it.

I hope other readers will support me in my wish to preserve this special place. *(190 words)*

PRACTICE TEST 4

Exercise 6 *(page 76)*

(Dear Sir/Madam,)

I am writing in response to your advertisement concerning building grants. I believe our town needs a new hospital. My family has lived here for nearly 20 years, and my brothers and I were born in our little hospital. The nursing staff there are friendly and efficient, but the hospital itself is really just a collection of small huts with no proper connecting corridors.

What our town needs is a large, modern hospital to cater for all the families that are now living in the new houses on the edge of the town. All the facilities – from operating theatres to the emergency department – need to be located on one site.

This new hospital could be built on the piece of land which was once the industrial area. It is convenient for access from the main road and is near the river, so the wards could have lovely views to cheer up sick patients.

I do hope that you will consider my suggestion. You will be helping many people by awarding us a grant for our much-needed hospital.

(Yours faithfully,) *(177 words)*

Exercise 7 *(page 78)*

Have you heard the news? Our college is planning to cut our music lessons and the orchestra and choir next year. What are your views about this decision?

Our music lessons fulfil many purposes. Firstly, the class is a team, singing and making music together. Secondly, we learn the theory of how music works and also its history – our teachers help us to appreciate music and to listen to a range of compositions. We even make up our own musical works.

Playing in the orchestra is also vital teamwork. It is fine to learn an instrument, but what is the point if it is not played in context with other instruments in an orchestra? Think of all the concerts we have held for parents this year – what would our college replace live music with?

Many of us enjoy singing in the choir and find it a relaxing contrast to academic study. Singing for the appreciation of an audience is satisfying too.

Some people say that this decision will allow extra time for subjects like English, but these extra lessons could take place during breaks or after school. We must keep our music, for the good of the college. *(198 words)*

Lightning Source UK Ltd.
Milton Keynes UK
UKOW07f0858040915

258065UK00001B/22/P